THE RAMAYANA

THE RAMAYANA

EPIC OF RAMA, PRINCE OF INDIA

ROMESH C. DUTT

GYAN

Published by

GYAN

Gyan Publishing House
5, Ansari Road
Daryaganj, New Delhi-110002
Phone: 011-47034999, 9811692060
E-mail: books@gyanbooks.com

Distribution Network
gyanbooks.com
India, USA, Canada, UK, Australia, France

ISBN: 978-81-212-8672-5 (PB)
First Published, 1899

2nd Impression 2023

Printed at: Gyan Press, Delhi.

THE RAMAYANA
Author: Romesh C. Dutt

THE RAMAYANA

EPIC OF RAMA, PRINCE OF INDIA

THE RAMAYANA

EPIC OF RAMA, PRINCE OF INDIA

Condensed into English Verse

By

ROMESH C. DUTT

KITABISTAN

ALLAHABAD

TO

THE RIGHT HON. PROFESSOR F. MAX MÜLLER

WHO HAS DEVOTED HIS LIFETIME TO THE ELUCIDATION OF

THE LEARNING, LITERATURE, AND RELIGION OF

ANCIENT INDIA

AND HAS RECOGNISED AND VINDICATED WHAT IS

TRUE AND GREAT AND ENNOBLING IN

MODERN INDIA

THIS TRANSLATION OF THE RAMAYANA

IS DEDICATED AS A

SINCERE TOKEN OF THE ESTEEM AND REGARD OF MY COUNTRYMEN

A NOTE ON

THE LATE ROMESH C. DUTT

Romesh Chunder Dutt, to whom English readers are indebted for the condensed metrical versions of the ancient Indian epics given in this volume, was one of the most distinguished sons of modern India. He came of a Hindu family standing high among the Kayasths, second of the great castes in Bengal, was born in 1848, and grew to manhood amid influences of deep spiritual disturbance. In those days an Indian youth who had felt the call of the West encountered the sternest opposition, from both his own family and the community, if he avowed his ambition of making the voyage to Europe. Romesh Dutt, having passed through the Presidency College, Calcutta, took his fate into his own hands. Accompanied by two friends, both of whom afterwards rose to eminence in Bengal, he secretly took ship, came to London, entered for the Indian Civil Service, and took third place in the open examination of 1869. He was the first of his race to attain the rank of divisional commissioner, and long before his retirement in 1897, at the end of twenty-five years' service, had made a high reputation as an administrator. He sat for a time in the Bengal Legislative Council, and, in recognition of his official work, received the Companionship of the Indian Empire. He died on November 30, 1909, at Baroda, the capital of the important Native State which he had served with brilliant success as revenue minister and dewan.

The influences which determined his literary activity were primarily European. As a student in Calcutta he had made acquaintance with the English classics, and later, while at University College, had read the poets insatiably. Nevertheless his first successes were achieved in his mother tongue. He wrote in Bengali, poems and plays, historical and social novels, and aroused a storm of protest within the orthodox community of his province by publishing a Bengali translation of the *Rig Veda*. In English, of which he had complete mastery, his first considerable essay was a history of Civilisation in Ancient India, which, though not a work of original research, fulfilled a useful purpose in its day. When freedom from Government service gave him the opportunity he set himself to writing the *Economic History of India* and *India in the Victorian Age*, the two together forming his chief contribution to the subject which he, more than any other Indian of his time, had made his own. In these books, as in others of kindred theme and purpose, there is much criticism of British administration, strongly felt if temperately expressed. Apart from this, its more controversial side, the work of Romesh Dutt is valuable mainly in that it has helped to reveal, to his own people no less than to ours, the spiritual riches of ancient India.

S. K. Ratcliffe

CONTENTS

Book		Page
I.	Sita-Swayamvara (*The Bridal of Sita*)	11
II.	Vana-Gamana-Adesa (*The Banishment*)	26
III.	Dasaratha-Viyoga (*The Death of the King*)	47
IV.	Rama-Bharata-Sambada (*The Meeting of the Princes*)	71
V.	Panchavati (*On the Banks of the Godavari*)	84
VI.	Sita-Harana (*Sita Lost*)	95
VII.	Kishkindha (*In the Nilgiri Mountains*)	110
VIII.	Sita Sandesa (*Sita Discovered*)	123
IX.	Ravana-Sabha (*The Council of War*)	131
X.	Yuddha (*The War in Ceylon*)	140
XI.	Rajya-Abhisheka (*Rama's Return and Consecration*)	164
XII.	Aswa-Medha (*Sacrifice of the Horse*)	173
	Conclusion	180
	Translator's Epilogue	182

BOOK I

SITA-SWAYAMVARA

(The Bridal of Sita)

The Epic relates to the ancient traditions of two powerful races, the Kosalas and the Videhas, who lived in Northern India between the twelfth and tenth centuries before Christ. The names Kosala and Videha in the singular number indicate the kingdoms,—Oudh and North Behar,—and in the plural number they mean the ancient races which inhabited those two countries.

According to the Epic, Dasa-ratha king of the Kosalas had four sons, the eldest of whom was Rama, the hero of the poem. And Janak, king of the Videhas, had a daughter named Sita, who was miraculously born of a field furrow, and who is the heroine of the Epic.

Janak ordained a severe test for the hand of his daughter, and many a prince and warrior came and went away disappointed. Rama succeeded, and won Sita. The story of Rama's winning his bride, and of the marriage of his three brothers with the sister and cousins of Sita, forms the subject of this Book.

The portions translated in this Book form Section vi., Sections lxvii to lxix., Section lxxiii., and Section lxxvii., of Book i of the original text.

I

AYODHYA, THE RIGHTEOUS CITY

Rich in royal worth and valour; rich in holy Vedic lore,
Dasa-ratha ruled his empire in the happy days of yore,

Loved of men in fair Ayodhya, sprung of ancient Solar Race,
Royal *rishi* in his duty, saintly *rishi* in his grace,

Great as INDRA in his prowess, bounteous as KUVERA kind,
Dauntless deeds subdued his foemen, lofty faith subdued his mind!

Like the ancient monarch Manu, father of the human race,
Dasa-ratha ruled his people with a father's loving grace,

Truth and Justice swayed each action and each baser motive quelled,
People's Love and Monarch's Duty every thought and deed impelled,

And his town like INDRA's city,—tower and dome and turret brave—
Rose in proud and peerless beauty on Sarayu's limpid wave!

Peaceful lived the righteous people, rich in wealth in merit high,
Envy dwelt not in their bosoms and their accents shaped no lie,

Fathers with their happy households owned their cattle, corn and gold,
Galling penury and famine in Ayodhya had no hold,

Neighbours lived in mutual kindness helpful with their ample wealth,
None who begged the wasted refuse, none who lived by fraud and
stealth!

And they wore the gem and earring, wreath and fragrant sandal paste,
And their arms were decked with bracelets, and their necks with
nishkas graced,

Cheat and braggart and deceiver lived not in the ancient town,
Proud despiser of the lowly wore not insults in their frown,

Poorer fed not on the richer, hireling friend upon the great,
None with low and lying accents did upon the proud man wait!

Men to plighted vows were faithful, faithful was each loving wife,
Impure thought and wandering fancy stained not holy wedded life,

Robed in gold and graceful garments, fair in form and fair in face,
Winsome were Ayodhya's daughters, rich in wit and woman's grace!

Twice-born men were free from passion, lust of gold and impure greed,
Faithful to their Rites and Scriptures, truthful in their word and deed,

Altar blazed in every mansion, from each home was bounty given,
Stooped no man to fulsome falsehood, questioned none the will of
Heaven.

Kshatras bowed to holy Brahmans, Vaisyas to the Kshatras bowed,
Toiling Sudras lived by labour, of their honest duty proud,

To the Gods and to the Fathers, to each guest in virtue trained,
Rites were done with due devotion as by holy writ ordained.

Pure each caste in due observance, stainless was each ancient rite,
And the nation thrived and prospered by its old and matchless might,

And each man in truth abiding lived a long and peaceful life,
With his sons and with his grandsons, with his loved and honoured wife.

Thus was ruled the ancient city by her monarch true and bold,
As the earth was ruled by Manu in the misty days of old,

Troops who never turned in battle, fierce as fire and strong and brave,
Guarded well her lofty ramparts as the lions guard the cave.

Steeds like INDRA's in their swiftness came from far Kamboja's land,
From Vanaya and Vahlika and from Sindhu's rock-bound strand,

Elephants of mighty stature from the Vindhya mountain came,
Or from deep and darksome forests round Himalay's peaks of fame,

Matchless in their mighty prowess, peerless in their wondrous speed,
Nobler than the noble tuskers sprung from high celestial breed.

Thus Ayodhya, "virgin city,"—faithful to her haughty name,—
Ruled by righteous Dasa-ratha won a world-embracing fame,

Strong-barred gates and lofty arches, tower and dome and turret high,
Decked the vast and peopled city fair as mansions of the sky.

Queens of proud and peerless beauty born of houses rich in fame,
Loved of royal Dasa-ratha to his happy mansion came,

Queen Kausalya blessed with virtue true and righteous Rama bore,
Queen Kaikeyi young and beauteous bore him Bharat rich in lore,

Queen Sumitra bore the bright twins, Lakshman and Satrughna bold,
Four brave princes served their father in the happy days of old!

II

Mithila, and the Breaking of the Bow

Janak monarch of Videha spake his message near and far,—
He shall win my peerless Sita who shall bend my bow of war,—

Suitors came from farthest regions, warlike princes known to fame,
Vainly strove to wield the weapon, left Videha in their shame.

Viswa-mitra royal *rishi*, Rama true and Lakshman bold,
Came to fair Mithila's city from Ayodhya famed of old,

Spake in pride the royal *rishi*: "Monarch of Videha's throne,
Grant, the wondrous bow of Rudra be to princely Rama shown."

Janak spake his royal mandate to his lords and warriors bold:
"Bring ye forth the bow of Rudra decked in garlands and in gold,"

And his peers and proud retainers waiting on the monarch's call,
Brought the great and goodly weapon from the city's inner hall.

Stalwart men of ample stature pulled the mighty iron car
In which rested all-inviolate Janak's dreaded bow of war,

And where midst assembled monarchs sat Videha's godlike king,
With a mighty toil and effort did the eight-wheeled chariot bring.

"This the weapon of Videha," proudly thus the peers begun,
"Be it shewn to royal Rama, Dasa-ratha's righteous son,"

"This the bow," then spake the monarch to the *rishi* famed of old,
To the true and righteous Rama and to Lakshman young and bold,

"This the weapon of my fathers prized by kings from age to age,
Mighty chiefs and sturdy warriors could not bend it, noble sage!

Gods before the bow of RUDRA have in righteous terror quailed,
Rakshas fierce and stout *Asuras* have in futile effort failed,

Mortal man will struggle vainly RUDRA's wondrous bow to bend,
Vainly strive to string the weapon and the shining dart to send,

Holy saint and royal *rishi*, here is Janak's ancient bow,
Shew it to Ayodhya's princes, speak to them my kingly vow !"

Vishwa-mitra humbly listened to the words the monarch said,
To the brave and righteous Rama, Janak's mighty bow displayed,

Rama lifted high the cover of the pond'rous iron car,
Gazed with conscious pride and prowess on the mighty bow of war.

"Let me," humbly spake the hero, "on this bow my fingers place,
Let me lift and bend the weapon, help me with your loving grace."

"Be it so," the *rishi* answered, "be it so," the monarch said,
Rama lifted high the weapon on his stalwart arms displayed,

Wond'ring gazed the kings assembled as the son of Raghu's race
Proudly raised the bow of RUDRA with a warrior's stately grace,

Proudly strung the bow of RUDRA which the kings had tried in vain,
Drew the cord with force resistless till the weapon snapped in twain !

Like the thunder's pealing accent rose the loud terrific clang,
And the firm earth shook and trembled and the hills in echoes rang,

And the chiefs and gathered monarchs fell and fainted in their fear,
And the men of many nations shook the dreadful sound to hear !

Pale and white the startled monarchs slowly from their terror woke,
And with royal grace and greetings Janak to the *rishi* spoke :

"Now my ancient eyes have witnessed wond'rous deed by Rama done,
Deed surpassing thought or fancy wrought by Dasa-ratha's son,

And the proud and peerless princess, Sita glory of my house,
Sheds on me an added lustre as she weds a godlike spouse,

True shall be my plighted promise, Sita dearer than my life,
Won by worth and wond'rous valour shall be Rama's faithful wife!

Grant us leave, O royal *rishi*, grant us blessings kind and fair,
Envoys mounted on my chariot to Ayodhya shall repair,

They shall speak to Rama's father glorious feat by Rama done,
They shall speak to Dasa-ratha, Sita is by valour won,

They shall say the noble princes safely live within our walls,
They shall ask him by his presence to adorn our palace halls!"

Pleased at heart the sage assented, envoys by the monarch sent,
To Ayodhya's distant city with the royal message went.

III

The Embassy to Ayodhya

Three nights halting in their journey with their steeds fatigued and spent,
Envoys from Mithila's monarch to Ayodhya's city went,

And by royal mandate bidden stepped within the palace hall,
Where the ancient Dasa-ratha sat with peers and courtiers all,

And with greetings and obeisance spake their message calm and bold,
Softly fell their gentle accents as their happy tale they told.

"Greetings to thee, mighty monarch, greetings to each priest and peer,
Wishes for thy health and safety from Videha's king we bear,

Janak monarch of Videha for thy happy life hath prayed,
And by Viswa-mitra's bidding words of gladsome message said:

'Known on earth my plighted promise, spoke by heralds near and far,—
He shall win my peerless Sita who shall bend my bow of war,—

Monarchs came and princely suitors, chiefs and warriors known to fame,
Baffled in their fruitless effort left Mithila in their shame,

Rama came with gallant Lakshman by their proud preceptor led,
Bent and broke the mighty weapon, he the beauteous bride shall wed!

Rama strained the weapon stoutly till it snapped and broke in twain,
In the concourse of the monarchs, in the throng of arméd men,

Rama wins the peerless princess by the righteous will of Heaven,
I redeem my plighted promise—be thy kind permission given!

Monarch of Kosala's country! with each lord and peer and priest,
Welcome to Mithila's city, welcome to Videha's feast,

Joy thee in thy Rama's triumph, joy thee with a father's pride,
Let each prince of proud Kosala win a fair Videha-bride!'

These by Viswa-mitra's bidding are the words our monarch said,
This by Sata-nanda's counsel is the quest that he hath made."

Joyful was Kosala's monarch, spake to chieftains in the hall,
Vama-deva and Vasishtha and to priests and Brahmans all:

"Priests and peers! in far Mithila, so these friendly envoys tell,
Righteous Rama, gallant Lakshman, in the royal palace dwell,

And our brother of Videha prizes Rama's warlike pride,
To each prince of proud Kosala yields a fair Videha-bride,

If it please ye, priests and chieftains, speed we to Mithila fair,
World-renowned is Janak's virtue, Heaven-inspired his learning rare!"

Spake each peer and holy Brahman: "Dasa-ratha's will be done!"
Spake the king unto the envoys: "Part we with the rising sun!"

Honoured with a regal honour, welcomed to a rich repast,
Gifted envoys from Mithila day and night in gladness passed!

2

IV

Meeting of Janak and Dasa-ratha

On Ayodhya's tower and turret now the golden morning woke,
Dasa-ratha girt by courtiers thus to wise Sumantra spoke:

"Bid the keepers of my treasure with their waggons lead the way,
Ride in front with royal riches, gold and gems in bright array,

Bid my warriors skilled in duty lead the four-fold ranks of war,
Elephants and noble chargers, serried foot and battle-car,

Bid my faithful chariot-driver harness quick each car of state,
With the fleetest of my coursers, and upon my orders wait.

Vama-deva and Vasishtha versed in *Veda's* ancient lore,
Kasyapa and good Jabali sprung from holy saints of yore,

Markandeya in his glory, Katyayana in his pride,
Let each priest and proud preceptor with Kosala's monarch ride,

Harness to my royal chariot strong and stately steeds of war,
For the envoys speed my journey and the way is long and far."

With each priest and proud retainer Dasa-ratha led the way,
Glittering ranks of forces followed in their four-fold dread array,

Four days on the way they journeyed till they reached Videha's land,
Janak with a courteous welcome came to greet the royal band.

Joyously Videha's monarch greeted every priest and peer,
Greeted ancient Dasa-ratha in his accents soft and clear:

"Hast thou come, my royal brother, on my house to yield thy grace,
Hast thou made a peaceful journey, pride of Raghu's royal race?

Welcome! for Mithila's people seek my royal guest to greet,
Welcome! for thy sons of valour long their loving sire to meet,

Welcome too the priest Vasishtha versed in *Veda's* ancient lore,
Welcome every righteous *rishi* sprung from holy saints of yore!

And my evil fates are vanquished and my race is sanctified,
With the warlike race of Raghu thus in loving bonds allied,

Sacrifice and rites auspicious we ordain with rising sun,
Ere the evening's darkness closes, happy nuptials shall be done !"

Thus in kind and courteous accents Janak spake his purpose high,
And his royal love responding, Dasa-ratha made reply :

"Gift betokens giver's bounty, —so our ancient sages sing,—
And thy righteous fame and virtue grace thy gift, Videha's king !

World-renowned is Janak's bounty, Heaven-inspired his holy grace,
And we take his boon and blessing as an honour to our race !"

Royal grace and kingly greetings marked the ancient monarch's word,
Janak with a grateful pleasure Dasa-ratha's answer heard,

And the Brahmans and preceptors joyously the midnight spent,
And in converse pure and pleasant and in sacred sweet content.

Righteous Rama gallant Lakshman piously their father greet,
Duly make their deep obeisance, humbly touch his royal feet,

And the night is filled with gladness for the king revered and old,
Honoured by the saintly Janak, greeted by his children bold,

On Mithila's tower and turret stars their silent vigils keep,
When each sacred rite completed, Janak seeks his nightly sleep.

V

The Preparation

All his four heroic princes now with Dasa-ratha stayed
In Mithila's ancient city, and their father's will obeyed,

Thither came the bold Yudhajit prince of proud Kaikeya's line,
On the day that Dasa-ratha made his gifts of gold and kine,

And he met the ancient monarch, for his health and safety prayed,
Made his bow and due obeisance and in gentle accents said :

"List, O king! my royal father, monarch of Kaikeya's race,
Sends his kindly love and greetings with his blessings and his grace,

And he asks if Dasa-ratha prospers in his wonted health,
If his friends and fond relations live in happiness and wealth.

Queen Kaikeyi is my sister, and to see her son I came,
Bharat prince of peerless virtue, worthy of his father's fame,

Aye, to see that youth of valour, by my royal father sent,
To Ayodhya's ancient city with an anxious heart I went,

In the city of Mithila,—thus did all thy subjects say,—
With his sons and with his kinsmen Dasa-ratha makes his stay,

Hence in haste I journeyed hither, travelling late and early dawn,
For to do thee due obeisance and to greet my sister's son!"

Spake the young and proud Kaikeya, dear and duly-greeted guest,
Dasa-ratha on his brother choicest gifts and honours pressed.

Brightly dawned the happy morning, and Kosala's king of fame,
With his sons and wise Vasishtha to the sacred *yajna* came,

Rama and his gallant brothers decked in gem and jewel bright,
In th' auspicious hour of morning did the blest *Kautuka* rite,

And beside their royal father piously the princes stood,
And to fair Videha's monarch spake Vasishtha wise and good:

"Dasa-ratha waits expectant with each proud and princely son,
Waits upon the bounteous giver, for each holy rite is done,

'Twixt the giver and the taker sacred word is sacred deed,
Seal with gift thy plighted promise, let the nuptial rites proceed!"

Thus the righteous-souled Vasishtha to Videha's monarch prayed,
Janak versed in holy *Vedas* thus in courteous accents said:

"Wherefore waits the king expectant? Free to him this royal dome,
Since my kingdom is his empire and my palace is his home,

And the maidens, flame-resplendent, done each fond *Kautuka* rite,
Beaming in their bridal beauty tread the sacrificial site!

I beside the lighted altar wait upon thy sacred hest,
And auspicious is the moment, sage Vasishtha knows the rest,

Let the peerless Dasa-ratha, proud Kosala's king of might,
With his sons and honoured sages enter on the holy site,

Let the righteous sage Vasishtha, sprung from Vedic saints of old,
Celebrate the happy wedding ; be the sacred *mantras* told !"

VI

The Wedding

Sage Vasishtha skilled in duty placed Videha's honoured king,
Viswa-mitra, Sata-nanda, all within the sacred ring,

And he raised the holy altar as the ancient writs ordain,
Decked and graced with scented garlands grateful unto gods and
men,

And he set the golden ladles, vases pierced by artists skilled,
Holy censers fresh and fragrant, cups with sacred honey filled,

Sanka bowls and shining salvers, *arghya* plates for honoured guest,
Parched rice arranged in dishes, corn unhusked that filled the rest,

And with careful hand Vasishtha grass around the altar flung,
Offered gift to lighted Agni and the sacred *mantra* sung !

Softly came the sweet-eyed Sita,—bridal blush upon her brow,—
Rama in his manly beauty came to take the sacred vow,

Janak placed his beauteous daughter facing Dasa-ratha's son,
Spake with father's fond emotion and the holy rite was done :

"*This is Sita child of Janak, dearer unto him than life,*
Henceforth sharer of thy virtue, be she, prince, thy faithful wife,

Of thy weal and woe partaker, be she thine in every land,
Cherish her in joy and sorrow, clasp her hand within thy hand,

As the shadow to the substance, to her lord is faithful wife,
And my Sita best of women follows thee in death or life !"

Tears bedew his ancient bosom, gods and men his wishes share,
And he sprinkles holy water on the blest and wedded pair.

Next he turned to Sita's sister, Urmila of beauty rare,
And to Lakshman young and valiant spake in accents soft and fair:

"*Lakshman, dauntless in thy duty, loved of men and Gods above,*
Take my dear devoted daughter, Urmila of stainless love,

Lakshman, fearless in thy virtue, take thy true and faithful wife,
Clasp her hand within thy fingers, be she thine in death or life!"

To his brother's child Mandavi, Janak turned with father's love,
Yielded her to righteous Bharat, prayed for blessings from above:

"*Bharat, take the fair Mandavi, be she thine in death or life,*
Clasp her hand within thy fingers as thy true and faithful wife!"

Last of all was Sruta-kriti, fair in form and fair in face,
And her gentle name was honoured for her acts of righteous grace

"*Take her by the hand, Satrughna, be she thine in death or life,*
As the shadow to the substance, to her lord is faithful wife!"

Then the princes held the maidens, hand embraced in loving hand
And Vasishtha spake the *mantra*, holiest priest in all the land,

And as ancient rite ordaineth, and as sacred laws require,
Stepped each bride and princely bridegroom round the altar's
lighted fire,

Round Videha's ancient monarch, round the holy *rishis* all,
Lightly stepped the gentle maidens, proudly stepped the princes
tall!

And a rain of flowers descended from the sky serene and fair,
And a soft celestial music filled the fresh and fragrant air,

Bright *Gandharvas* skilled in music waked the sweet celestial song,
Fair *Apsaras* in their beauty on the green sward tripped along!

As the flowery rain descended and the music rose in pride,
Thrice around the lighted altar every bridegroom led his bride,

And the nuptial rites were ended, princes took their brides away,
Janak followed with his courtiers, and the town was proud and gay!

VII

Return to Ayodhya

With his wedded sons and daughters and his guard in bright array,
To the famed and fair Ayodhya, Dasa-ratha held his way,

And they reached the ancient city decked with banners bright and brave,
And the voice of drum and trumpet hailed the home-returning brave.

Fragrant blossoms strewed the pathway, song of welcome filled the air,
Joyous men and merry women issued forth in garments fair,

And they lifted up their faces and they waved their hands on high,
And they raised the voice of welcome as their righteous king drew nigh.

Greeted by his loving subjects, welcomed by his priests of fame,
Dasa-ratha with the princes to his happy city came,

With the brides and stately princes in the town he held his way,
Entered slow his lofty palace bright as peak of Himalay.

Queen Kausalya blessed with virtue, Queen Kaikeyi in her pride,
Queen Sumitra sweetly loving, greeted every happy bride,

Soft-eyed Sita noble-destined, Urmila of spotless fame,
Mandavi and Sruta-kriti to their loving mothers came.

Decked in silk and queenly garments they performed each pious rite,
Brought their blessings on the household, bowed to Gods of holy might,

Bowed to all the honoured elders, blest the children with their love,
And with soft and sweet endearment by their loving consorts moved.

Happy were the wedded princes peerless in their warlike might,
And they dwelt in stately mansions like KUVERA's mansions bright,

Loving wife and troops of kinsmen, wealth and glory on them wait,
Filial love and fond affection sanctify their happy fate.

Once when on the palace chambers bright the golden morning
woke,
To his son the gentle Bharat, thus the ancient monarch spoke :

"Know, my son, the prince Kaikeya, Yudajit of warlike fame,
Queen Kaikeyi's honoured brother, from his distant regions came,

He hath come to take thee, Bharat, to Kaikeya's monarch bold,
Go and stay with them a season, greet thy grandsire loved of old."

Bharat heard with filial duty and he hastened to obey,
Took with him the young Satrughna in his grandsire's home to
stay,

And from Rama and from Lakshman parted they with many a tear,
From their young and gentle consorts, from their parents ever
dear,

And Kaikeya with the princes, with his guards and troopers gay,
To his father's western regions gladsome held his onward way.

Rama with a pious duty,—favoured by the Gods above,—
Tended still his ancient father with a never-faltering love,

In his father's sacred mandate still his noblest Duty saw,
In the weal of subject nations recognised his foremost law !

And he pleased his happy mother with a fond and filial care,
And his elder and his kinsmen with devotion soft and fair,

Brahmans blessed the righteous Rama for his faith in gods above,
People in the town and hamlet blessed him with their loyal love !

With a woman's whole affection fond and trusting Sita loved,
And within her faithful bosom loving Rama lived and moved,

And he loved her, for their parents chose her as his faithful wife,
Loved her for her peerless beauty, for her true and trustful life,

Loved and dwelt within her bosom though he wore a form apart,
Rama in a sweet communion lived in Sita's loving heart !

Days of joy and months of gladness o'er the gentle Sita flew,
As she like the QUEEN OF BEAUTY brighter in her graces grew,

And as VISHNU with his consort dwells in skies, alone, apart,
Rama in a sweet communion lived in Sita's loving heart !

BOOK II

VANA-GAMANA-ADESA

(The Banishment)

The events narrated in this Book occupy scarcely two days. The description of Rama's princely virtues and the rejoicings at his proposed coronation, with which the Book begins, contrast with much dramatic force and effect with the dark intrigues which follow, and which end in his cruel banishment for fourteen years.

The portions translated in this Book form Sections i., ii., vi., and vii., portions of Sections x. to xiii., and the whole of Section xviii. of Book ii. of the original text.

I

The Council Convened

Thus the young and brave Satrughna, Bharat ever true and bold,
Went to warlike western regions where Kaikeyas lived of old,

Where the ancient Aswa-pati ruled his kingdom broad and fair,
Hailed the sons of Dasa-ratha with a grandsire's loving care.

Tended with a fond affection, guarded with a gentle sway,
Still the princes of their father dreamt and thought by night and day,

And their father in Ayodhya, great of heart and stout of hand,
Thought of Bharat and Satrughna living in Kaikeya's land.

For his great and gallant princes were to him his life and light,
Were a part of Dasa-ratha like his hands and arms of might,

But of all his righteous children righteous Rama won his heart,
As Swayambhu of all creatures, was his dearest, holiest part,

For his Rama strong and stately was his eldest and his best,
Void of every baser passion and with every virtue blest !

Soft in speech, sedate and peaceful, seeking still the holy path,
Calm in conscious worth and valour, taunt nor cavil waked his
wrath,

In the field of war excelling, boldest warrior midst the bold,
In the palace chambers musing on the tales by elders told,

Faithful to the wise and learned, truthful in his deed and word,
Rama dearly loved his people and his people loved their lord !

To the Brahmans pure and holy Rama due obeisance made,
To the poor and to the helpless deeper love and honour paid,

Spirit of his race and nation was to high-souled Rama given,
Thoughts that widen human glory, deeds that ope the gates of
heaven !

Not intent on idle cavil Rama spake with purpose high,
And the God of speech might envy when he spake or made reply,

In the learning of the *Vedas* highest meed and glory won,
In the skill of arms the father scarcely matched the gallant son !

Taught by sages and by elders in the manners of his race,
Rama grew in social virtues and each soft endearing grace,

Taught by inborn pride and wisdom patient purpose to conceal,
Deep determined was his effort, dauntless was his silent will !

Peerless in his skill and valour steed and elephant to tame,
Dauntless leader of his forces, matchless in his warlike fame,

Higher thought and nobler duty did the righteous Rama move,
By his toil and by his virtues still he sought his people's love !

Dasa-ratha marked his Rama with each kingly virtue blest,
And from life-long royal duties now he sought repose and rest :

"Shall I see my son anointed, seated on Kosala's throne,
In the evening of my life-time ere my days on earth be done,

Shall I place my ancient empire in the youthful Rama's care,
Seek for me a higher duty and prepare for life more fair?"

Pondering thus within his bosom counsel from his courtiers sought,
And to crown his Rama, Regent, was his purpose and his thought,

For strange signs and diverse tokens now appeared on earth and sky,
And his failing strength and vigour spoke his end approaching nigh,

And he witnessed Rama's virtues filling all the world with love,
As the full-moon's radiant lustre fills the earth from skies above!

Dear to him appeared his purpose, Rama to his people dear,
Private wish and public duty made his path serene and clear,

Dasa-ratha called his Council, summoned chiefs from town and plain,
Welcomed too from distant regions monarchs and the kings of men,

Mansions meet for prince and chieftain to his guests the monarch gave,
Gracious as the Lord of Creatures held the gathering rich and brave!

Nathless to Kosala's Council nor Videha's monarch came,
Nor the warlike chief Kaikeya, Aswa-pati king of fame,

To those kings and near relations, ancient Dasa-ratha meant,
Message of the proud anointment with his greetings would be sent.

Brightly dawned the day of gathering; in the lofty Council Hall,
Stately chiefs and ancient burghers came and mustered one and all,

And each prince and peer was seated on his cushion rich and high,
And on monarch Dasa-ratha eager turned his anxious eye,

Girt by crownéd kings and chieftains, burghers from the town and plain,
Dasa-ratha shone like INDRA girt by heaven's immortal train!

II

The People Consulted

With the voice of pealing thunder Dasa-ratha spake to all,
To the princes and the burghers gathered in Ayodhya's hall:

"Known to all, the race of Raghu rules this empire broad and fair,
And hath ever loved and cherished subjects with a father's care,

In my fathers' footsteps treading I have sought the ancient path,
Nursed my people as my children, free from passion, pride and wrath,

Underneath this white umbrella, seated on this royal throne,
I have toiled to win their welfare and my task is almost done!

Years have passed of fruitful labour, years of work by fortune blest,
And the evening of my life-time needs, my friends, the evening's rest,

Years have passed in watchful effort, Law and Duty to uphold,
Effort needing strength and prowess,—and my feeble limbs are old!

Peers and burghers, let your monarch, now his lifelong labour done,
For the weal of loving subjects on his empire seat his son,

INDRA-like in peerless valour, *rishi*-like in holy lore,
Rama follows Dasa-ratha, but in virtues stands before!

Throned in Pushya's constellation shines the moon with fuller light,
Throned to rule his father's empire Rama wins a loftier might,

He will be your gracious monarch favoured well by FORTUNE'S QUEEN,
By his virtues and his valour lord of earth he might have been!

Speak your thought and from this bosom lift a load of toil and care,
On the proud throne of my fathers let me place a peerless heir,

Speak your thought, my chiefs and people, if this purpose please you well,
Or if wiser, better counsel in your wisdom ye can tell,

Speak your thought without compulsion, though this plan to me be dear,
If some middle course were wiser, if some other way were clear!"

Gathered chieftains hailed the mandate with applauses long and loud,
As the peafowls hail the thunder of the dark and laden cloud,

And the gathered subjects echoed loud and long the welcome sound,
Till the voices of the people shook the sky and solid ground!

Brahmans versed in laws of duty, chieftains in their warlike pride,
Countless men from town and hamlet heard the mandate far and wide,

And they met in consultation, joyously with one accord,
Freely and in measured accents, gave their answer to their lord:

"Years of toil and watchful labour weigh upon thee, king of men,
Young in years is righteous Rama, Heir and Regent let him reign,

We would see the princely Rama, Heir and Regent duly made,
Riding on the royal tusker in the white umbrella's shade!"

Searching still their secret purpose, seeking still their thought to know,
Spake again the ancient monarch in his measured words and slow:

"I would know your inner feelings, loyal thoughts and whispers kind,
For a doubt within me lingers and a shadow clouds my mind,

True to Law and true to Duty while I rule this kingdom fair,
Wherefore would you see my Rama seated as the Regent Heir?"

"We would see him Heir and Regent, Dasa-ratha, ancient lord,
For his heart is blessed with valour, virtue marks his deed and word,

Lives not man in all the wide-earth who excels the stainless youth,
In his loyalty to Duty, in his love of righteous Truth,

Truth impels his thought and action, Truth inspires his soul with grace,
And his virtue fills the wide earth and exalts his ancient race!

Bright Immortals know his valour; with his brother Lakshman bold,
He hath never failed to conquer hostile town or castled hold,

And returning from his battles, from the duties of the war,
Riding on his royal tusker of his all-resistless car,

As a father to his children to his loving men he came,
Blessed our homes and maids and matrons till our infants lisped his name,

For our humble woes and troubles Rama hath the ready tear,
To our humble tales of suffering Rama lends his willing ear!

Happy is the royal father who hath such a righteous son,
For in town and mart and hamlet every heart hath Rama won,

Burghers and the toiling tillers tales of Rama's kindness say,
Man and infant, maid and matron, morn and eve for Rama pray,

To the Gods and bright Immortals we our inmost wishes send,
May the good and godlike Rama on his father's throne ascend,

Great in gifts and great in glory, Rama doth our homage own,
We would see the princely Rama seated on his father's throne!"

III

The City Decorated

With his consort pious Rama, pure in deed and pure in thought,
After evening's due ablutions Narayana's chamber sought,

Prayed unto the Lord of Creatures, Narayana Ancient Sire,
Placed his offering on his forehead, poured it on the lighted fire,

Piously partook the remnant, sought for Narayana's aid,
As he kept his fast and vigils on the grass of *kusa* spread.

With her lord the saintly Sita silent passed the sacred night,
Contemplating World's Preserver, Lord of Heaven's ethereal height,

And within the sacred chamber on the grass of *kusa* lay,
Till the crimson streaks of morning ushered in the festive day,

Till the royal bards and minstrels chanted forth the morning call,
Pealing through the holy chamber, echoing through the royal hall.

Past the night of sacred vigils, in his silken robes arrayed,
Message of the proud anointment Rama to the Brahmans said,

And the Brahmans spake to burghers that the festive day was come,
Till the mart and crowded pathway rang with note of pipe and drum,

And the townsmen heard rejoicing of the vigils of the night,
Kept by Rama and by Sita for the day's auspicious rite.

Rama shall be Heir and Regent, Rama shall be crowned to-day,—
Rapid flew the gladdening message with the morning's gladsome ray,

And the people of the city, maid and matron, man and boy,
Decorated fair Ayodhya in their wild tumultuous joy!

On the temple's lofty steeple high as cloud above the air,
On the crossing of the pathways, in the garden green and fair,

On the merchant's ample warehouse, on the shop with stores displayed,
On the mansion of the noble by the cunning artist made,

On the gay and bright pavilion, on the high and shady trees,
Banners rose and glittering streamers, flags that fluttered in the breeze!

Actors gay and nimble dancers, singers skilled in lightsome song,
With their antics and their music pleased the gay and gathered throng,

And the people met in conclaves, spake of Rama, Regent Heir,
And the children by the road-side lisped of Rama brave and fair !

Women wove the scented garland, merry maids the censer lit,
Men with broom and sprinkled water swept the spacious mart and street,

Rows of trees and posts they planted hung with lamps for coming night,
That the midnight dark might rival splendour of the noonday light!

Troops of men and merry children laboured with a loving care,
Woman's skill and woman's fancy made the city passing fair,

So that good and kindly Rama might his people's toil approve,
So that sweet and soft-eyed Sita might accept her people's love !

Groups of joyous townsmen gathered in the square or lofty hall,
Praised the monarch Dasa-ratha, regent Rama young and tall :

"Great and good is Dasa-ratha born of Raghu's royal race,
In the fulness of his lifetime on his son he grants his grace,

And we hail the rite auspicious for our prince of peerless might,
He will guard us by his valour, he will save our cherished right,

Dear unto his loving brothers in his father's palace hall,
As is Rama to his brothers dear is Rama to us all,

Long live ancient Dasa-ratha king of Raghu's royal race,
We shall see his son anointed by his father's righteous grace !"

Thus of Rama's consecration spake the burghers one and all,
And the men from distant hamlets poured within the city wall,

From the confines of the empire, north and south and west and east,
Came to see the consecration and to share the royal feast !

And the rolling tide of nations raised their voices loud and high,
Like the tide of sounding ocean when the full moon lights the sky,

And Ayodhya thronged by people from the hamlet, mart and lea,
Was tumultuous like the ocean thronged by creatures of the sea !

IV

Intrigue

In the inner palace chamber stood the proud and peerless queen,
With a mother's joy Kaikeyi gaily watched the festive scene,

But with deep and deadly hatred Manthara, her nurse and maid,
Marked the city bright with banners, and in scornful accents said :

"Take thy presents back, Kaikeyi, for they ill befit the day,
And when clouds of sorrow darken, ill beseems thee to be gay,

And thy folly moves my laughter though an anguish wakes my sigh,
For a gladness stirs thy bosom when thy greatest woe is nigh !

Who that hath a woman's wisdom, who that is a prudent wife,
Smiles in joy when prouder rival triumphs in the race of life,

How can hapless Queen Kaikeyi greet this deed of darkness done,
When the favoured Queen Kausalya wins the empire for her son ?

Know the truth, O witless woman ! Bharat is unmatched in fame,
Rama, deep and darkly jealous, dreads thy Bharat's rival claim,

Younger Lakshman with devotion doth on eldest Rama wait,
Young Satrughna with affection follows Bharat's lofty fate,

Rama dreads no rising danger from the twins, the youngest-born,
But thy Bharat's claims and virtues fill his jealous heart with scorn !

Trust me, queen, thy Bharat's merits are too well and widely known,
And he stands too near and closely by a rival brother's throne,

Rama hath a wolf-like wisdom and a fang to reach the foe,
And I tremble for thy Bharat, Heaven avert untimely woe !

Happy is the Queen Kausalya, they will soon anoint her son,
When on Pushya's constellation gaily rides to-morrow's moon,

Happy is the Queen Kausalya in her regal pomp and state,
And Kaikeyi like a bond-slave must upon her rival wait !

Wilt thou do her due obeisance as we humble women do,
Will thy proud and princely Bharat as his brother's henchman go,

Will thy Bharat's gentle consort, fairest princess in this land,
In her tears and in her anguish wait on Sita's proud command ?"

With a woman's scornful anger Manthara proclaimed her grief,
With a mother's love for Rama thus Kaikeyi answered brief:

"What inspires thee, wicked woman, thus to rail in bitter tone,
Shall not Rama, best and eldest, fill his father's royal throne,

What alarms thee, crooked woman, in the happy rites begun,
Shall not Rama guard his brothers as a father guards his son ?

And when Rama's reign is over, shall not Gods my Bharat speed,
And by law and ancient custom shall not younger son succeed,

In the present bliss of Rama and in Bharat's future hope,
What offends thee, senseless woman, wherefore dost thou idly mope ?

Dear is Rama as my Bharat, ever duteous in his ways,
Rama honours Queen Kausalya, loftier honour to me pays,

Rama's realm is Bharat's kingdom, ruling partners they shall prove,
For himself than for his brothers Rama owns no deeper love !"

Scorn and anger shook her person and her bosom heaved a sigh,
As in wilder, fiercer accents Manthara thus made reply:

"What insensate rage or madness clouds thy heart and blinds thine eye,
Courting thus thy own disaster, courting danger dread and high,

What dark folly clouds thy vision to the workings of thy foe,
Heedless thus to seek destruction and to sink in gulf of woe ?

Know, fair queen, by law and custom, son ascends the throne of pride,
Rama's son succeedeth Rama, luckless Bharat steps aside,

Brothers do not share a kingdom, nor can one by one succeed,
Mighty were the civil discord if such custom were decreed !

For to stop all war and tumult, thus the ancient laws ordain,
Eldest son succeeds his father, younger children may not reign,

Bharat barred from Rama's empire, vainly decked with royal grace,
Friendless, joyless, long shall wander, alien from his land and race!

Thou hast borne the princely Bharat, nursed him from thy gentle breast,
To a queen and to a mother need a prince's claims be pressed,

To a thoughtless heedless mother must I Bharat's virtues plead,
Must the Queen Kaikeyi witness Queen Kausalya's son succeed?

Trust thy old and faithful woman who hath nursed thee, youthful queen,
And in great and princely houses many darksome deeds hath seen,

Trust my word, the wily Rama for his spacious empire's good,
Soon will banish friendless Bharat and secure his peace with blood!

Thou hast sent the righteous Bharat to thy ancient father's land,
And Satrughna young and valiant doth beside his brother stand,

Young in years and generous-hearted, they will grow in mutual love,
As the love of elder Rama doth in Lakshman's bosom move.

Young companions grow in friendship, and our ancient legends tell,
Weeds protect a forest monarch which the woodman's axe would fell,

Crownéd Rama unto Lakshman will a loving brother prove,
But for Bharat and Satrughna, Rama's bosom owns no love,

And a danger thus ariseth if the elder wins the throne,
Haste thee, heedless Queen Kaikeyi, save the younger and thy son!

Speak thy mandate to thy husband, let thy Bharat rule at home,
In the deep and pathless jungle let the banished Rama roam,

This will please thy ancient father and thy father's kith and kin,
This will please the righteous people, Bharat knows no guile or sin!

Speak thy mandate to thy husband, win thy son a happy fate,
Doom him not to Rama's service or his unrelenting hate,

Let not Rama in his rancour shed a younger brother's blood,
As the lion slays the tiger in the deep and echoing wood !

With the magic of thy beauty thou hast won thy monarch's heart,
Queen Kausalya's bosom rankles with a woman's secret smart,

Let her not with woman's vengeance turn upon her prouder foe,
And as crownéd Rama's mother venge her in Kaikeyi's woe,

Mark my word, my child Kaikeyi, much these ancient eyes have seen,
Rama's rule is death to Bharat, insult to my honoured queen !"

Like a slow but deadly poison worked the ancient nurse's tears,
And a wife's undying impulse mingled with a mother's fears,

Deep within Kaikeyi's bosom worked a woman's jealous thought,
Speechless in her scorn and anger mourner's dark retreat she sought.

V

The Queen's Demand

Rama shall be crowned at sunrise, so did royal bards proclaim,
Every rite arranged and ordered, Dasa-ratha homeward came,

To the fairest of his consorts, dearest to his ancient heart,
Came the king with eager gladness joyful message to impart,

Radiant as the Lord of Midnight, ere the eclipse casts its gloom,
Came the old and ardent monarch heedless of his darksome doom !

Through the shady palace garden where the peacock wandered free,
Lute and lyre poured forth their music, parrot flew from tree to tree,

Through the corridor of creepers, painted rooms by artists done,
And the halls where scented *Champak* and the flaming *Asok* shone,

Through the portico of splendour graced by silver, tusk and gold,
Radiant with his thought of gladness walked the monarch proud
and bold.

Through the lines of scented blossoms which by limpid waters
shone,
And the rooms with seats of silver, ivory bench and golden throne,

Through the chamber of confection, where each viand wooed the
taste,
Every object in profusion as in regions of the blest,

Through Kaikeyi's inner closet lighted with a softened sheen,
Walked the king with eager longing,—but Kaikeyi was not seen!

Thoughts of love and gentle dalliance woke within his ancient heart,
And the magic of her beauty and the glamour of her art,

With a soft desire the monarch vainly searched the vanished fair,
Found her not in royal chamber, found her not in gay parterre!

Filled with love and longing languor loitered not the radiant queen,
In her soft voluptuous chamber, in the garden, grove or green,

And he asked the faithful warder of Kaikeyi loved and lost,
She who served him with devotion and his wishes never crost,

Spake the warder in his terror that the queen with rage distraught,
Weeping silent tears of anguish had the mourner's chamber sought!

Thither flew the stricken monarch; on the bare and unswept
ground,
Trembling with tumultuous passion was the Queen Kaikeyi found,

On the cold uncovered pavement sorrowing lay the weeping wife,
Young wife of an ancient husband, dearer than his heart and life!

Like a bright and blossoming creeper rudely severed from the
earth,
Like a fallen fair *Apsara*, beauteous nymph of heavenly birth,

Like a female forest-ranger bleeding from the hunter's dart,
Whom her mate the forest-monarch soothes with soft endearing art,

Lay the queen in tears of anguish ! And with sweet and gentle word,
To the lotus-eyed lady, softly spake her loving lord :

"Wherefore thus, my Queen and Empress, sorrow-laden is thy heart,
Who with daring slight or insult seeks to cause thy bosom smart ?

If some unknown ailment pains thee, evil spirit of the air,
Skilled physicians wait upon thee, priests with incantations fair,

If from human foe some insult, wipe thy tears and doom his fate,
Rich reward or royal vengeance shall upon thy mandate wait !

Wilt thou doom to death the guiltless, free whom direst sins debase,
Wilt thou lift the poor and lowly or the proud and great disgrace,

Speak, and I and all my courtiers Queen Kaikeyi's hest obey,
For thy might is boundless, Empress, limitless thy regal sway !

Rolls my chariot-wheel revolving from the sea to farthest sea,
And the wide earth is my empire, monarchs list my proud decree,

Nations of the eastern regions and of Sindhu's western wave,
Brave Saurashtras and the races who the ocean's dangers brave,

Vangas, Angas and Magadhas, warlike Matsyas of the west,
Kasis and the southern races, brave Kosalas first and best,

Nations of my world-wide empire, rich in corn and sheep and kine,
All shall serve my Queen Kaikeyi and their treasures all are thine,

Speak, command thy king's obedience, and thy wrath will melt away,
Like the melting snow of winter 'neath the sun's reviving ray !"

Blinded was the ancient husband as he lifted up her head,
Heedless oath and word he plighted that her wish should be obeyed,

Scheming for a fatal purpose, inly then Kaikeyi smiled,
And by sacred oath and promise bound the monarch love-beguiled :

"Thou hast given, Dasa-ratha, troth and word and royal oath,
Three and thirty Gods be witness, watchers of the righteous truth,

Sun and Moon and Stars be witness, Sky and Day and sable Night,
Rolling Worlds and this our wide Earth, and each dark and unseen wight,

Witness Rangers of the forest, Household Gods that guard us both,
Mortal beings and Immortal,—witness ye the monarch's oath,

Ever faithful to his promise, ever truthful in his word,
Dasa-ratha grants my prayer, Spirits and the Gods have heard !

Call to mind, O righteous monarch, days when in a bygone strife,
Warring with thy foes immortal thou hadst almost lost thy life,

With a woman's loving tendance poor Kaikeyi cured thy wound,
Till from death and danger rescued, thou wert by a promise bound,

Two rewards my husband offered, what my loving heart might seek,
Long delayed their wished fulfilment,—now let poor Kaikeyi speak,

And if royal deeds redeem not what thy royal lips did say,
Victim to thy broken promise Queen Kaikeyi dies to-day !

By these rites ordained for Rama,—such the news my menials bring,—
Let my Bharat, and not Rama, be anointed Regent King,

Wearing skins and matted tresses, in the cave or hermit's cell,
Fourteen years in Dandak's forests let the elder Rama dwell,

These are Queen Kaikeyi's wishes, these are boons for which I pray,
I would see my son anointed, Rama banished on this day !"

VI

The King's Lament

"Is this torturing dream or madness, do my feeble senses fail,
O'er my darkened mind and bosom doth a fainting fit prevail ?"

So the stricken monarch pondered and in hushed and silent fear,
Looked on her as on a tigress looks the dazed and stricken deer,

Lying on the unswept pavement still he heaved the choking sigh,
Like a wild and hissing serpent quelled by incantations high !

Sobs convulsive shook his bosom and his speech and accent failed,
And a dark and deathlike faintness o'er his feeble soul prevailed,

Stunned awhile remained the monarch, then in furious passion woke,
And his eyeballs flamed with redfire, to the queen as thus he spoke :

"Traitress to thy king and husband, fell destroyer of thy race,
Wherefore seeks thy ruthless rancour Rama rich in righteous grace,

Traitress to thy kith and kindred, Rama loves thee as thy own,
Wherefore then with causeless vengeance as a mother hate thy son ?

Have I courted thee, Kaikeyi, throned thee in my heart of truth,
Nursed thee in my home and bosom like a snake of poisoned tooth,

Have I courted thee, Kaikeyi, placed thee on Ayodhya's throne,
That my Rama, loved of people, thou shouldst banish from his own ?

Banish far my Queen Kausalya, Queen Sumitra saintly wife,
Wrench from me my ancient empire, from my bosom wrench my life,

But with brave and princely Rama never can his father part,
Till his ancient life is ended, cold and still his beating heart !

Sunless roll the world in darkness, rainless may the harvests thrive,
But from righteous Rama severed, never can his sire survive,

Feeble is thy aged husband, few and brief on earth his day,
Lend me, wife, a woman's kindness, as a consort be my stay !

Ask for other boon, Kaikeyi, aught my sea-girt empire yields,
Wealth or treasure, gem or jewel, castled town or smiling fields,

Ask for other gift, Kaikeyi, and thy wishes shall be given,
Stain me not with crime unholy in the eye of righteous Heaven !"

Coldly spake the Queen Kaikeyi : "If thy royal heart repent,
Break thy word and plighted promise, let thy royal faith be rent,

Ever known for truth and virtue, speak to peers and monarchs all,
When from near and distant regions they shall gather in thy hall,

Speak if so it please thee, monarch, of thy evil-destined wife,
How she loved with wife's devotion, how she served and saved
thy life,

How on plighted promise trusting for a humble boon she sighed,
How a monarch broke his promise, how a cheated woman died!"

"Fair thy form," resumed the monarch, "beauty dwells upon thy
face,
Woman's winsome charms bedeck thee, and a woman's peerless
grace,

Wherefore then within thy bosom wakes this thought of cruel wile,
And what dark and loathsome spirit stains thy heart with blackest
guile?

Ever since the day, Kaikeyi, when a gentle bride you came,
By a wife's unfailing duty you have won a woman's fame,

Wherefore now this cruel purpose hath a stainless heart defiled,
Ruthless wish to send my Rama to the dark and pathless wild?

Wherefore, darkly-scheming woman, on unrighteous purpose bent,
Doth thy cruel causeless vengeance on my Rama seek a vent,

Wherefore seek by deeds unholy for thy son the throne to win,
Throne which Bharat doth not covet,—blackened by his mother's
sin?

Shall I see my banished Rama mantled in the garb of woe,
Reft of home and kin and empire to the pathless jungle go,

Shall I see disasters sweeping o'er my empire dark and deep,
As the forces of a foeman o'er a scattered army sweep?

Shall I hear assembled monarchs in their whispered voices say,
Weak and foolish in his dotage, Dasa-ratha holds his sway,

Shall I say to righteous elders when they blame my action done,
That by woman's mandate driven I have banished thus my son?

Queen Kausalya, dear-loved woman! she who serves me as a slave
Soothes me like a tender sister, helps me like a consort brave,

As a fond and loving mother tends me with a watchful care,
As a daughter ever duteous doth obeisance sweet and fair,

When my fond and fair Kausalya asks me of her banished son,
How shall Dasa-ratha answer for the impious action done,

How can husband, cold and cruel, break a wife's confiding heart,
How can father, false and faithless, from his best and eldest part?"

Coldly spake the Queen Kaikeyi: "If thy royal heart repent,
Break thy word and plighted promise, let thy royal faith be rent,

Truth-abiding is our monarch, so I heard the people say,
And his word is all inviolate, stainless virtue marks his sway,

Let it now be known to nations,—righteous Dasa-ratha lied,
And a trusting, cheated woman broke her loving heart and died!"

Darker grew the shades of midnight, coldly shone each distant star,
Wilder in the monarch's bosom raged the struggle and the war:

"Starry midnight, robed in shadows! give my wearied heart relief,
Spread thy sable covering mantle o'er an impious monarch's grief,

Spread thy vast and inky darkness o'er a deed of nameless crime,
Reign perennial o'er my sorrows heedless of the lapse of time,

May a sinful monarch perish ere the dawning of the day,
O'er a dark life sin-polluted, beam not morning's righteous ray!"

VII

The Sentence

Morning came and duteous Rama to the palace bent his way,
For to make his salutation and his due obeisance pay,

And he saw his aged father shorn of kingly pomp and pride,
And he saw the Queen Kaikeyi sitting by her consort's side.

Duteously the righteous Rama touched the ancient monarch's feet,
Touched the feet of Queen Kaikeyi with son's obeisance meet.

"Rama!" cried the feeble monarch, but the tear bedimmed his eye,
Sorrow choked his failing utterance and his bosom heaved a sigh,

Rama started in his terror at his father's grief or wrath,
Like a traveller in the jungle crossed by serpent in his path!

Reft of sense appeared the monarch, crushed beneath a load of pain,
Heaving oft a sigh of sorrow as his heart would break in twain,

Like the ocean tempest-shaken, like the sun in eclipse pale,
Like a crushed repenting *rishi* when his truth and virtue fail!

Breathless mused the anxious Rama,—what foul action hath he done,
What strange anger fills his father, wherefore greets he not his son?

"Speak, my mother," uttered Rama, "what strange error on my part,
Unremembered sin or folly fills with grief my father's heart,

Gracious unto me is father with a father's boundless grace,
Wherefore clouds his altered visage, wherefore tears bedew his face?

Doth a piercing painful ailment rack his limbs with cruel smart,
Doth some secret silent anguish wring his torn and tortured heart,

Bharat lives with brave Satrughna in thy father's realms afar,
Hath some cloud of dark disaster crossed their bright auspicious star?

Duteously the royal consorts on the loving monarch wait,
Hath some woe or dire misfortune dimmed the lustre of their fate,

I would yield my life and fortune ere I wound my father's heart,
Hath my unknown crime or folly caused his ancient bosom smart?

Ever dear is Queen Kaikeyi to her consort and her king,
Hath some angry accent escaped thee thus his royal heart to wring,

Speak, my ever-loving mother, speak the truth for thou must know,
What distress or deep disaster pains his heart and clouds his brow?"

Mother's love nor woman's pity moved the deep-determined queen,
As in cold and cruel accents thus she spake her purpose keen:

"Grief nor woe nor sudden ailment pains thy father loved of old,
But he fears to speak his purpose to his Rama true and bold,

And his loving accents falter some unloving wish to tell,
Till you give your princely promise, you will serve his mandate well!

Listen more, in bygone seasons,—Rama thou wert then unborn,—
I had saved thy royal father, he a gracious boon had sworn,

But his feeble heart repenting is by pride and passion stirred,
He would break his royal promise as a caitiff breaks his word,

Years have passed and now the monarch would his ancient word forego,
He would build a needless causeway when the waters ceased to flow!

Truth inspires each deed attempted and each word by monarchs spoke,
Not for thee, though loved and honoured, should a royal vow be broke,

If the true and righteous Rama binds him by his father's vow,
I will tell thee of the anguish which obscures his royal brow,

If thy feeble bosom falter and thy halting purpose fail,
Unredeemed is royal promise and unspoken is my tale!"

"Speak thy word," exclaimed the hero, "and my purpose shall not fail,
Rama serves his father's mandate and his bosom shall not quail,

Poisoned cup or death untimely,—what the cruel fates decree,—
To his king and to his father Rama yields obedience free,

Speak my father's royal promise, hold me by his promise tied,
Rama speaks and shall not palter, for his lips have never lied."

Cold and clear Kaikeyi's accents fell as falls the hunter's knife,
"Listen then to word of promise and redeem it with thy life,

Wounded erst by foes immortal, saved by Queen Kaikeyi's care,
Two great boons your father plighted and his royal words were fair,

I have sought their due fulfilment,—brightly shines my Bharat's star,—
Bharat shall be Heir and Regent, Rama shall be banished far!

If thy father's royal mandate thou wouldst list and honour still,
Fourteen years in Dandak's forest live and wander at thy will,

Seven long years and seven, my Rama, thou shalt in the jungle dwell,
Bark of trees shall be thy raiment and thy home the hermit's cell,

Over fair Kosala's empire let my princely Bharat reign,
With his cars and steeds and tuskers, wealth and gold and armed men!

Tender-hearted is the monarch, age and sorrow dim his eye,
And the anguish of a father checks his speech and purpose high,

For the love he bears thee, Rama, cruel vow he may not speak,
I have spoke his will and mandate, and thy true obedience seek."

Calmly Rama heard the mandate, grief nor anger touched his heart,
Calmly from his father's empire and his home prepared to part.

BOOK III

DASA-RATHA-VIYOGA

(*The Death of the King*)

The first six days of Rama's wanderings are narrated in this Book. Sita and the faithful Lakshman accompanied Rama in his exile, and the loyal people of Ayodhya followed their exiled prince as far as the banks of the Tamasa river where they halted on the first night. Rama had to steal away at night to escape the citizens, and his wanderings during the following days give us beautiful glimpses of forest life in holy hermitages. Thirty centuries have passed since the age of the Kosalas and Videhas, but every step of the supposed journey of Rama is well known in India to this day, and is annually traversed by thousands of devoted pilgrims. The past is not dead and buried in India, it lives in the hearts of millions of faithful men and faithful women, and shall live for ever.

On the third day of their exile, Rama and his wife and brother crossed the Ganges; on the fourth day they came to the hermitage of Bharad-vaja, which stood where Allahabad now stands, on the confluence of the Ganges and the Jumna; on the fifth day they crossed the Jumna, the southern shores of which were then covered with woods; and on the sixth day they came to the hill of Chitra-kuta, where they met the saint Valmiki, the reputed author of this Epic. "We have often looked," says a writer in *Calcutta Review*, vol. xxii, "on that green hill: it is the holiest spot of that sect of the Hindu faith who devote themselves to this incarnation of Vishnu. The whole neighbourhood is Rama's country. Every headland has some legend, every cavern is connected with his name, some of the wild fruits are still called Sita-phal, being the reputed food of the exile. Thousands and thousands annually visit the spot, and round the hill is raised a footpath on which the devotee, with naked feet treads full of pious awe."

Grief for the banished Rama pressed on the ancient heart of Dasa-ratha. The feeble old king pined away and died, remembering and recounting on his death-bed how in his youth he had caused sorrow and death to an old hermit by killing his son. Scarcely any passage in the Epic is more touching than this old sad story told by the dying monarch.

The portions translated in this Book form the whole or the main portions of Sections xxvi., xxvii., xxxi., xxxix., xl., xlvi., lii., liv., lv., lvi., lxiii., and lxiv. of Book ii. of the original text.

I

Woman's Love

"Dearly loved, devoted Sita! daughter of a royal line,
Part we now, for years of wand'ring in the pathless woods is mine,

For my father, promise-fettered, to Kaikeyi yields the sway,
And she wills her son anointed,—fourteen years doth Rama stray,

But before I leave thee, Sita, in the wilderness to rove,
Yield me one more tender token of thy true and trustful love!

Serve my crowned brother, Sita, as a faithful duteous dame,
Tell him not of Rama's virtues, tell him not of Rama's claim,

Since my royal father willeth,—Bharat shall be regent-heir,
Serve him with a loyal duty, serve him with obeisance fair,

Since my royal father willeth,—years of banishment be mine,
Brave in sorrow and in suffering, woman's brightest fame be thine!

Keep thy fasts and vigils, Sita, while thy Rama is away,
Faith in Gods and faith in virtue on thy bosom hold their sway,

In the early watch of morning to the Gods for blessings pray,
To my father Dasa-ratha honour and obeisance pay,

To my mother, Queen Kausalya, is thy dearest tendance due,
Offer her thy consolation, be a daughter fond and true!

Queen Kaikeyi and Sumitra equal love and honour claim,
With a soothing soft endearment sweetly serve each royal dame,

Cherish Bharat and Satrughna with a sister's watchful love,
And a mother's true affection and a mother's kindness prove !

Listen, Sita, unto Bharat speak no heedless angry word,
He is monarch of Kosala and of Raghu's race is lord,

Crownéd kings our willing service and our faithful duty own,
Dearest sons they disinherit, cherish strangers near the throne !

Bharat's will with deep devotion and with faultless faith obey,
Truth and virtue on thy bosom ever hold their gentle sway,

And to please each dear relation, gentle Sita, be it thine,
Part we love ! for years of wand'ring in the pathless woods is
mine !"

Rama spake, and soft-eyed Sita, ever sweet in speech and word,
Stirred by loving woman's passion boldly answered thus her lord :

"Do I hear my husband rightly, are these words my Rama spake,
And her banished lord and husband will the wedded wife
forsake ?

Lightly I dismiss the counsel which my lord hath lightly said,
For it ill beseems a warrior and my husband's princely grade !

For the faithful woman follows where her wedded lord may lead,
In the banishment of Rama, Sita's exile is decreed,

Sire nor son nor loving brother rules the wedded woman's state,
With her lord she falls or rises, with her consort courts her fate,

If the righteous son of Raghu wends to forests dark and drear,
Sita steps before her husband wild and thorny paths to clear !

Like the tasted refuse water cast thy timid thoughts aside,
Take me to the pathless jungle, bid me by my lord abide,

Car and steed and gilded palace, vain are these to woman's life,
Dearer is her husband's shadow to the loved and loving wife !

For my mother often taught me and my father often spake,
That her home the wedded woman doth beside her husband make,

As the shadow to the substance, to her lord is faithful wife,
And she parts not from her consort till she parts with fleeting life!

Therefore bid me seek the jungle and in pathless forests roam,
Where the wild deer freely ranges and the tiger makes his home,

Happier than in father's mansions in the woods will Sita rove,
Waste no thought on home or kindred, nestling in her husband's
love!

World-renowned is Rama's valour, fearless by her Rama's side,
Sita still will live and wander with a faithful woman's pride,

And the wild fruit she will gather from the fresh and fragrant wood,
And the food by Rama tasted shall be Sita's cherished food!

Bid me seek the sylvan greenwoods, wooded hills and plateaus high,
Limpid rills and crystal *nullas* as they softly ripple by,

And where in the lake of lotus tuneful ducks their plumage lave,
Let me with my loving Rama skim the cool translucent wave!

Years will pass in happy union,—happiest lot to woman given,—
Sita seeks not throne or empire, nor the brighter joys of heaven,

Heaven conceals not brighter mansions in its sunny fields of pride,
Where without her lord and husband faithful Sita would reside!

Therefore let me seek the jungle where the jungle-rangers rove,
Dearer than the royal palace, where I share my husband's love,

And my heart in sweet communion shall my Rama's wishes share,
And my wifely toil shall lighten Rama's load of woe and care!"

Vainly gentle Rama pleaded dangers of the jungle life,
Vainly spake of toil and trial to a true and tender wife!

II

Brother's Faithfulness

Tears bedewed the face of Lakshman as he heard what Sita said,
And he touched the feet of Rama and in gentle accents prayed:

"If my elder and his lady to the pathless forests wend,
Armed with bow and ample quiver Lakshman will on them attend,

Where the wild deer range the forest and the lordly tuskers roam,
And the bird of gorgeous plumage nestles in its jungle home,

Dearer far to me those woodlands where my elder Rama dwells,
Than the homes of bright Immortals where perennial bliss prevails!

Grant me then thy sweet permission,—faithful to thy glorious star,
Lakshman shall not wait and tarry when his Rama wanders far,

Grant me then thy loving mandate,—Lakshman hath no wish to stay,
None shall bar the faithful younger when the elder leads the way!"

"Ever true to deeds of virtue, duteous brother, faithful friend,
Dearer than his life to Rama, thou shalt not to forests wend,

Who shall stay by Queen Kausalya, Lakshman, if we both depart,
Who shall stay by Queen Sumitra, she who nursed thee on her heart?

For the king our aged father, he who ruled the earth and main,
Is a captive to Kaikeyi, fettered by her silken chain,

Little help Kaikeyi renders to our mothers in her pride,
Little help can Bharat offer, standing by his mother's side.

Thou alone can'st serve Kausalya when for distant woods I part,
When the memory of my exile rankles in her sorrowing heart,

Thou alone can'st serve Sumitra, soothe her sorrows with thy love,
Stay by them, my faithful Lakshman, and thy filial virtues prove,

Be this then thy sacred duty, tend our mothers in their woe,
Little joy or consolation have they left on earth below!"

Spake the hero: "Fear no evil, well is Rama's prowess known,
And to mighty Rama's mother Bharat will obeisance own,

Nathless if the pride of empire sways him from the righteous path,
Blood will venge the offered insult and will quench our filial wrath!

But a thousand peopled hamlets Queen Kausalya's hests obey,
And a thousand armèd champions own her high and queenly sway,

Aye, a thousand village-centres Queen Sumitra's state maintain,
And a thousand swords like Lakshman's guard her proud and prosperous reign!

All alone with gentle Sita thou shalt track thy darksome way,
Grant it, that thy faithful Lakshman shall protect her night and day,

Grant it, with his bow and quiver Lakshman shall the forests roam,
And his axe shall fell the jungle, and his hands shall rear the home!

Grant it, in the deepest woodlands he shall seek the forest fruit,
Berries dear to holy hermits and the sweet and luscious root,

And when with thy meek-eyed Sita thou shalt seek the mountain crest,
Grant it, Lakshman ever duteous watch and guard thy nightly rest!"

Words of brother's deep devotion Rama heard with grateful heart,
And with Sita and with Lakshman for the woods prepared to part:

"Part we then from loving kinsmen, arms and mighty weapons bring,
Bows of war which Lord VARUNA rendered to Videha's king,

Coats of mail to sword impervious, quivers which can never fail,
And the rapiers bright as sunshine, golden-hilted, tempered well,

Safely rest these goodly weapons in our great preceptor's hall,
Seek and bring them, faithful brother, for methinks we need them all!"

Rama spake; his valiant brother then the wondrous weapons brought
Wreathed with fresh and fragrant garlands and with gold and jewels wrought,

"Welcome, brother," uttered Rama, "stronger thus to woods we go,
Wealth and gold and useless treasure to the holy priests bestow,

To the son of saint Vasishtha, to each sage is honour due,
Then we leave our father's mansions, to our father's mandate true!"

III

Mother's Blessings

Tears of sorrow and of suffering flowed from Queen Kausalya's eye,
As she saw departing Sita for her blessings drawing nigh,

And she clasped the gentle Sita and she kissed her moistened head,
And her tears like summer tempest choked the loving words she said:

"Part we, dear devoted daughter, to thy husband ever true,
With a woman's whole affection render love to husband's due!

False are women loved and cherished, gentle in their speech and word,
When misfortune's shadows gather, who are faithless to their lord,

Who through years of sunny splendour smile and pass the livelong day,
When misfortune's darkness thickens, from their husband turn away,

Who with changeful fortune changing oft ignore the plighted word,
And forget a woman's duty, woman's faith to wedded lord,

Who to holy love inconstant from their wedded consort part,
Manly deed nor manly virtue wins the changeful woman's heart!

But the true and righteous woman, loving spouse and changeless wife,
Faithful to her lord and consort holds him dearer than her life,

Ever true and righteous Sita, follow still my godlike son,
Like a God to thee is Rama in the woods or on the throne!"

"I shall do my duty, mother," said the wife with wifely pride,
"Like a God to me is Rama, Sita shall not leave his side,

From the Moon will part his lustre ere I part from wedded lord,
Ere from faithful wife's devotion falter in my deed or word,

For the stringless lute is silent, idle is the wheel-less car,
And no wife the loveless consort, inauspicious is her star!

Small the measure of affection which the sire and brother prove,
Measureless to wedded woman is her lord and husband's love,

True to Law and true to Scriptures, true to woman's plighted word,
Can I ever be, my mother, faithless, loveless to my lord?"

Tears of joy and mingled sorrow filled the Queen Kausalya's eye,
As she marked the faithful Sita true in heart, in virtue high,

And she wept the tears of sadness when with sweet obeisance due,
Spake with hands in meekness folded Rama ever good and true:

"Sorrow not, my loving mother, trust in virtue's changeless beam,
Swift will fly the years of exile like a brief and transient dream,

Girt by faithful friends and forces, blest by righteous Gods above,
Thou shalt see thy son returning to thy bosom and thy love!"

Unto all the royal ladies Rama his obeisance paid,
For his failings unremembered, blessings and forgiveness prayed,

And his words were soft and gentle, and they wept to see him go,
Like the piercing cry of curlew rose the piercing voice of woe,

And in halls where drum and tabor rose in joy and regal pride,
Voice of grief and lamentation sounded far and sounded wide!

Then the true and faithful Lakshman parted from each weeping
dame,
And to sorrowing Queen Sumitra with his due obeisance came,

And he bowed to Queen Sumitra and his mother kissed his head,
Stilled her anguish-laden bosom and in trembling accents said:

"Dear devoted duteous Lakshman, ever to thy elder true,
When thy elder wends to forest, forest-life to thee is due,

Thou hast served him true and faithful in his glory and his fame,
This is Law for true and righteous,—serve him in his woe and
shame,

This is Law for race of Raghu known on earth for holy might,
Bounteous in their sacred duty, brave and warlike in the fight!

Therefore tend him as thy father, as thy mother tend his wife,
And to thee, like fair Ayodhya be thy humble forest life,

Go, my son, the voice of Duty bids my gallant Lakshman go,
Serve thy elder with devotion and with valour meet thy foe!"

IV

Citizens' Lament

Spake Sumantra chariot-driver waiting by the royal car,
"Haste thee, mighty-destined Rama, for we wander long and far,

Fourteen years in Dandak's forest shall the righteous Rama stray,
Such is Dasa-ratha's mandate, haste thee Rama and obey."

Queenly Sita bright-apparelled, with a strong and trusting heart,
Mounted on the car of splendour for the pathless woods to part,

And the king for needs providing gave her robes and precious store,
For the many years of exile in a far and unknown shore,

And a wealth of warlike weapons to the exiled princes gave,
Bow and dart and linkéd armour, sword and shield and lances brave.

Then the gallant brothers mounted on the gold-emblazoned car,
For unending was the journey and the wilderness was far,

Skilled Sumantra saw them seated, urged the swiftly-flying steed,
Faster than the speed of tempest was the noble coursers' speed.

And they parted for the forest; like a long unending night,
Gloomy shades of grief and sadness deepened on the city's might,

Mute and dumb but conscious creatures felt the woe the city bore,
Horses neighed and shook their bright bells, elephants returned a roar!

Man and boy and maid and matron followed Rama with their eye,
As the thirsty seek the water when the parchéd fields are dry,

Clinging to the rapid chariot, by its side, before, behind,
Thronging men and wailing women wept for Rama good and kind:

"Draw the reins, benign Sumantra, slowly drive the royal car,
We would once more see our Rama banished long and banished far,

Iron-hearted is Kausalya from her Rama thus to part,
Rends it not her mother's bosom thus to see her son depart?

True is righteous-hearted Sita cleaving to her husband still,
As the ever present sunlight cleaves to Meru's golden hill,

Faithful and heroic Lakshman! thou hast by thy brother stood,
And in duty still unchanging thou hast sought the pathless wood,

Fixed in purpose, true in valour, mighty boon to thee is given,
And the narrow path thou choosest is the righteous path to heaven!"

Thus they spake in tears and anguish as they followed him apace,
And their eyes were fixed on Rama, pride of Raghu's royal race,

Meanwhile ancient Dasa-ratha from his palace chamber came,
With each weeping queen and consort, with each woe-distracted dame!

And around the aged monarch rose the piercing voice of pain,
Like the wail of forest creatures when the forest-king is slain,

And the faint and feeble monarch was with age and anguish pale,
Like the darkened moon at eclipse when his light and radiance fail!

Rama saw his ancient father with a faltering footstep go,
Used to royal pomp and splendour, stricken now by age and woe,

Saw his mother faint and feeble to the speeding chariot hie,
As the mother-cow returneth to her young that loiters by,

Still she hastened to the chariot, "Rama! Rama!" was her cry,
And a throb was in her bosom and a tear was in her eye!

"Speed, Sumantra," uttered Rama, "from this torture let me part,
Speed, my friend, this sight of sadness breaks a much-enduring heart,

Heed not Dasa-ratha's mandate, stop not for the royal train,
Parting slow is lengthened sorrow like the sinner's lengthened pain!"

Sad Sumantra urged the coursers and the rapid chariot flew,
And the royal chiefs and courtiers round their fainting monarch drew,

And they spake to Dasa-ratha: "Follow not thy banished son,
He whom thou wouldst keep beside thee comes not till his task is done!"

Dasa-ratha, faint and feeble, listened to these words of pain,
Stood and saw his son departing,—saw him not on earth again!

V

Crossing the Tamasa : The Citizens' Return

Evening's thickening shades descended on Tamasa's distant shore,
Rama rested by the river, day of toilsome journey o'er,

And Ayodhya's loving people by the limpid river lay,
Sad and sorrowing they had followed Rama's chariot through the day!

"Soft-eyed Sita, faithful Lakshman," thus the gentle Rama said,
"Hail the first night of our exile mantling us in welcome shade,

Weeps the lone and voiceless forest, and in darksome lair and nest,
Feathered bird and forest creature seek their midnight's wonted rest,

Weeps methinks our fair Ayodhya to her Rama ever dear,
And perchance her men and women shed for us a silent tear,

Loyal men and faithful women, they have loved their ancient king,
And his anguish and our exile will their gentle bosoms wring!

Most I sorrow for my father and my mother loved and lost,
Stricken by untimely anguish, by a cruel fortune crost,

But the good and righteous Bharat gently will my parents tend,
And with fond and filial duty tender consolation lend,

Well I know his stainless bosom and his virtues rare and high,
He will soothe our parents' sorrow and their trickling tear will dry!

Faithful Lakshman, thou hast nobly stood by us when sorrows fell,
Guard my Sita by thy valour, by thy virtues tend her well,

Wait on her while from this river Rama seeks his thirst to slake,
On this first night of his exile food nor fruit shall Rama take,

Thou Sumantra, tend the horses, darkness comes with close of day,
Weary was the endless journey, weary is our onward way!"

Store of grass and welcome fodder to the steeds the driver gave,
Gave them rest and gave them water from Tamasa's limpid wave,

And performing night's devotions, for the princes made their bed,
By the softly rippling river 'neath the tree's umbrageous shade.

On a bed of leaf and verdure Rama and his Sita slept,
Faithful Lakshman with Sumantra nightly watch and vigils kept,

And the stars their silent lustre on the weary exiles shed,
And on wood and rolling river night her darksome mantle spread,

Early woke the righteous Rama and to watchful Lakshman spake,
"Mark the slumb'ring city people, still their nightly rest they take,

They have left their homes and children, followed us with loyal
heart,
They would take us to Ayodhya, from their princes loth to part!

Speed, my brother, for the people wake not till the morning's star,
Speed by night the silent chariot, we may travel fast and far,

So my true and loving people see us not by dawn of day,
Follow not through wood and jungle Rama in his onward way,

For a monarch meek in suffering should his burden bravely bear,
And his true and faithful people may not ask his woe to share!"

Lakshman heard the gentle mandate, and Sumantra yoked the steed,
Fresh with rest and grateful fodder, matchless in their wondrous
speed,

Rama with his gentle consort and with Lakshman true and brave,
Crossed beneath the silent starlight dark Tamasa's limpid wave.

On the further bank a pathway, fair to view and far and wide,
Stretching onwards to the forest spanned the spacious country side,

"Leave the broad and open pathway," so the gentle Rama said,
"Follow yet a track diverging, so the people be misled,.

Then returning to the pathway we shall march ere break of day,
So our true and faithful people shall not know our southward way."

Wise Sumantra hastened northward, then returning to the road,
By his master and his consort and the valiant Lakshman stood,

Raghu's sons and gentle Sita mounted on the stately car,
And Sumantra drove the coursers travelling fast and travelling far.

Morning dawned, the waking people by Tamasa's limpid wave,
Saw not Rama and his consort, saw not Lakshman young and brave,

And the tear suffused their faces and their hearts with anguish burned,
Sorrow-laden and lamenting to their cheerless homes returned.

VI

Crossing the Ganges. Bharad-Vaja's Hermitage

Morning dawned, and far they wandered, by their people loved and lost,
Drove through grove and flowering woodland, rippling rill and river crost,

Crossed the sacred Vedasruti on their still unending way,
Crossed the deep and rapid Gumti where the herds of cattle stray,

All the toilsome day they travelled, evening fell o'er wood and lea,
And they came where sea-like Ganga rolls in regal majesty,

'Neath a tall Ingudi's shadow by the river's zephyrs blest,
Second night of Rama's exile passed in sleep and gentle rest.

Morning dawned, the royal chariot Rama would no further own,
Sent Sumantra and the coursers back to fair Ayodhya's town,

Doffing then their royal garments Rama and his brother bold,
Coats of bark and matted tresses wore like anchorites of old.

Guha, chief of wild Nishadas, boat and needed succour gave,
And the princes and fair Sita ventured on the sacred wave,

And by royal Rama bidden strong Nishadas plied the oar,
And the strong boat quickly bounding left fair Ganga's northern shore.

"Goddess of the mighty Ganga !" so the pious Sita prayed,
"Exiled by his father's mandate, Rama seeks the forest shade,

Ganga ! o'er the three worlds rolling, bride and empress of the sea,
And from BRAHMA's sphere descended ! banished Sita bows to thee,

May my lord return in safety, and a thousand fattened kine,
Gold and gifts and gorgeous garments, pure libations shall be thine,

And with flesh and corn I worship unseen dwellers on thy shore,
May my lord return in safety, fourteen years of exile o'er !"

On the southern shore they journeyed through the long and weary day,
Still through grove and flowering woodland held their long and weary way,

And they slayed the deer of jungle and they spread their rich repast,
Third night of the princes' exile underneath a tree was past.

Morning dawned, the soft-eyed Sita wandered with the princes brave,
To the spot where ruddy Ganga mingles with dark Jumna's wave,

And they crost the shady woodland, verdant lawn and grassy mead,
Till the sun was in its zenith, Rama then to Lakshman said :

"Yonder mark the famed Prayaga, spot revered from age to age,
And the line of smoke ascending speaks some *rishi's* hermitage,

There the waves of ruddy Ganga with the dark blue Jumna meet,
And my ear the sea-like voices of the mingling waters greet.

Mark the monarchs of the forest severed by the hermit's might,
And the logs of wood and fuel for the sacrificial rite,

Mark the tall trees in their blossom and the peaceful shady grove,
There the sages make their dwelling, thither, Lakshman, let us rove."

Slowly came the exile-wand'rers, when the sun withdrew his rays,
Where the vast and sea-like rivers met in sisters' sweet embrace,

And the *Asram's* peaceful dwellers, bird of song and spotted deer,
Quaked to see the princely strangers in their warlike garb appear!

Rama stepped with valiant Lakshman, gentle Sita followed close,
Till behind the screening foliage hermits' peaceful dwellings rose,

And they came to Bharad-vaja, anchorite and holy saint,
Girt by true and faithful pupils on his sacred duty bent.

Famed for rites and lofty penance was the anchorite of yore,
Blest with more than mortal vision, deep in more than mortal lore,

And he sat beside the altar for the *agni-hotra* rite,
Rama spake in humble accents to the man of holy might:

"We are sons of Dasa-ratha and to thee our homage bring,
With my wife, the saintly Sita, daughter of Videha's king.

Exiled by my royal father in the wilderness I roam,
And my wife and faithful brother make the pathless woods their home,

We would through these years of exile in some holy *asram* dwell,
And our food shall be the wild fruit and our drink from crystal well,

We would practise pious penance still on sacred rites intent,
Till our souls be filled with wisdom and our years of exile spent!"

Pleased the ancient Bharad-vaja heard the prince's humble tale,
And with kind and courteous welcome royal strangers greeted well,

And he brought the milk and *arghya* where the guests observant stood,
Crystal water from the fountain, berries from the darksome wood,

And a low and leafy cottage for their dwelling-place assigned,
As a host receives a stranger, welcomed them with offerings kind.

In the *asram's* peaceful courtyard fearless browsed the jungle deer,
All unharmed the bird of forest pecked the grain collected near,

And by holy men surrounded 'neath the trees' umbrageous shade,
In his pure and peaceful accents *rishi* Bharad-vaja said :

"Not unknown or unexpected, princely strangers, have ye come,
I have heard of sinless Rama's causeless banishment from home,

Welcome to a hermit's forest, be this spot your place of rest,
Where the meeting of the rivers makes our sacred *asram* blest,

Live amidst these peaceful woodlands, still on sacred rites intent,
Till your souls be filled with wisdom and your years of exile spent !"

"Gracious are thy accents, *rishi*," Rama answered thus the sage,
"But fair towns and peopled hamlets border on this hermitage,

And to see the banished Sita and to see us, much I fear,
Crowds of rustics oft will trespass on thy calm devotions here,

Far from towns and peopled hamlets, grant us, *rishi*, in thy grace,
Some wild spot where hid in jungle we may pass these years in peace."

"Twenty miles from this Prayaga," spake the *rishi* pond'ring well,
"Is a lonely hill and jungle where some ancient hermits dwell,

Chitra-kuta, Peak of Beauty, where the forest creatures stray,
And in every bush and thicket herds of lightsome monkeys play,

Men who view its towering summit are on lofty thoughts inclined,
Earthly pride nor earthly passions cloud their pure and peaceful mind,

Hoary-headed ancient hermits, hundred autumns who have done,
By their faith and lofty penance heaven's eternal bliss have won,

Holy is the fair seclusion for thy purpose suited well,
Or if still thy heart inclineth, here in peace and comfort dwell!"

Spake the *rishi* Bharad-vaja, and with every courteous rite,
Cheered his guests with varied converse till the silent hours of
night,

Fourth night of the princes' exile in Prayaga's hermitage,
Passed the brothers and fair Sita honoured by Prayaga's Sage.

VII

Crossing the Jumna—Valmiki's Hermitage

Morning dawned, and faithful Sita with the brothers held her way,
Where the dark and eddying waters of the sacred Jumna stray,

Pondering by the rapid river long the thoughtful brothers stood,
Then with stalwart arms and axes felled the sturdy jungle wood,

Usira of strongest fibre, slender bamboo smooth and plain,
Jambu branches intertwining with the bent and twisting cane,

And a mighty raft constructed, and with creepers scented sweet,
Lakshman for the gentle Sita made a soft and pleasant seat.

Then the rustic bark was floated, framed with skill of woodman's craft,
By her loving lord supported Sita stepped upon the raft,

And her raiments and apparel Rama by his consort laid,
And the axes and the deerskins, bow and dart and shining blade,

Then with stalwart arms the brothers plied the bending bamboo oar,
And the strong raft gaily bounding left for Jumna's southern shore.

"Goddess of the glorious Jumna!" so the pious Sita prayed,
"Peaceful be my husband's exile in the forest's darksome shade,

May he safely reach Ayodhya, and a thousand fattened kine,
Hundred jars of sweet libation, mighty Jumna, shall be thine,

Grant that from the woods returning he may see his home again,
Grant that honoured by his kinsmen he may rule his loving men !"

On her breast her arms she folded while the princes plied the oar,
And the bright bark bravely bounding reached the wooded southern shore.

And the wanderers from Ayodhya on the river's margin stood,
Where the unknown realm extended mantled by unending wood,

Gallant Lakshman with his weapons went before the path to clear,
Soft-eyed Sita followed gently, Rama followed in the rear.

Oft from tree and darksome jungle, Lakshman ever true and brave,
Plucked the fruit or smiling blossom and to gentle Sita gave,

Oft to Rama turned his consort, pleased and curious evermore,
Asked the name of tree or creeper, fruit or flower unseen before.

Still with brotherly affection Lakshman brought each dewy spray,
Bud or blossom of wild beauty from the woodland bright and gay,

Still with eager joy and pleasure Sita turned her eye once more,
Where the tuneful swans and *saras* flocked on Jumna's sandy shore.

Two miles thus they walked and wandered and the belt of forest passed,
Slew the wild deer of the jungle, spread on leaves their rich repast,

Peacocks flew around them gaily, monkeys leaped on branches bent,
Fifth night of their endless wanderings in the forest thus they spent.

"Wake, my love, and list the warblings and the voices of the wood,"
Thus spake Rama when the morning on the eastern mountains stood,

Sita woke and gallant Lakshman, and they sipped the sacred wave,
To the hill of Chitra-kuta held their way serene and brave.

"Mark, my love," so Rama uttered, "every bush and tree and flower,
Tinged by radiant light of morning sparkles in a golden shower,

Mark the flaming flower of *Kinsuk* and the *Vilwa* in its pride,
Luscious fruits in wild profusion ample store of food provide,

Mark the honeycombs suspended from each tall and stately tree,
How from every virgin blossom steals her store the faithless bee!

Oft the lone and startled wild cock sounds its clarion full and clear,
And from flowering fragrant forests peacocks send the answering cheer,

Oft the elephant of jungle ranges in this darksome wood,
For yon peak is Chitra-kuta loved by saints and hermits good,

Oft the chanted songs of hermits echo through its sacred grove,
Peaceful on its shady uplands, Sita, we shall live and rove!"

Gently thus the princes wandered through the fair and woodland scene,
Fruits and blossoms lit the branches, feathered songsters filled the green,

Anchorites and ancient hermits lived in every sylvan grove,
And a sweet and sacred stillness filled the woods with peace and love!

Gently thus the princes wandered to the holy hermitage,
Where in lofty contemplation lived the mighty Saint and Sage,

Heaven inspired thy song, Valmiki! Ancient Bard of Ancient day,
Deeds of virtue and of valour live in thy undying lay!

And the Bard received the princes with a father's greetings kind,
Bade them live in Chitra-kuta with a pure and peaceful mind,

To the true and faithful Lakshman, Rama then his purpose said,
And of leaf and forest timber Lakshman soon a cottage made,

"So our sacred *Sastras* sanction," thus the righteous Rama spake,
"Holy offering we should render when our dwelling-home we make,

Slay the black buck, gallant Lakshman, and a sacrifice prepare,
For the moment is auspicious and the day is bright and fair."

Lakshman slew a mighty black-buck, with the antlered trophy came,
Placed the carcass consecrated by the altar's blazing flame,

Radiant round the mighty offering tongues of red fire curling shone,
And the buck was duly roasted and the tender meat was done.

Pure from bath, with sacred *mantra* Rama did the holy rite,
And invoked the bright Immortals for to bless the dwelling site,

To the kindly VISWA-DEVAS, and to RUDRA fierce and strong,
And to VISHNU Lord of Creatures, Rama raised the sacred song.

Righteous rite was duly rendered for the forest-dwelling made,
And with true and deep devotion was the sacred *mantra* prayed,

And the worship of the Bright Ones purified each earthly stain,
Pure-souled Rama raised the altar and the *Chaitya's* sacred fane.

Evening spread its holy stillness, bush and tree its magic felt,
As the Gods in BRAHMA's mansions, exiles in their cottage dwelt,

In the woods of Chitra-kuta where the Malyavati flows,
Sixth day of their weary wand'rings ended in a sweet repose.

VIII

TALE OF THE HERMIT'S SON

Wise Sumantra chariot-driver came from Ganga's sacred wave,
And unto Ayodhya's monarch, banished Rama's message gave,

Dasa-ratha's heart was shadowed by the deepening shade of night,
As the darkness of the eclipse glooms the sun's meridian light!

On the sixth night,—when his Rama slept in Chitra-kuta's bower,—
Memory of an ancient sorrow flung on him its fatal power,

Of an ancient crime and anguish, unforgotten, dark and dread,
Through the lapse of years and seasons casting back its death-like shade!

And the gloom of midnight deepened, Dasa-ratha sinking fast,
To Kausalya sad and sorrowing spake his memories of the past:

"Deeds we do in life, Kausalya, be they bitter, be they sweet,
Bring their fruit and retribution, rich reward or suffering meet,

Heedless child is he, Kausalya, in his fate who doth not scan,
Retribution of his *karma*, sequence of a mighty plan!

Oft in madness and in folly we destroy the mango grove,
Plant the gorgeous gay *palasa* for the red flower that we love,

Fruitless as the red *palasa* is the *karma* I have sown,
And my barren lifetime withers through the deed which is my own!

Listen to my tale, Kausalya, in my days of youth renowned,
I was called a *sabda-bedhi*, archer prince who shot by sound,

I could hit the unseen target, by the sound my aim could tell,—
Blindly drinks a child the poison, blindly in my pride I fell!

I was then my father's Regent, thou a maid to me unknown,
Hunting by the fair Sarayu in my car I drove alone,

Buffalo or jungle tusker might frequent the river's brink,
Nimble deer or watchful tiger stealing for his nightly drink,

Stalking with a hunter's patience, loitering in the forests drear,
Sound of something in the water struck my keen and listening ear,

In the dark I stood and listened, some wild beast the water drunk,
'Tis some elephant, I pondered, lifting water with its trunk.

I was called a *sabda-bedhi*, archer prince who shot by sound,
On the unseen fancied tusker dealt a sure and deadly wound,

Ah! too deadly was my arrow and like hissing cobra fell,
On my startled ear and bosom smote a voice of human wail,

Dying voice of lamentation rose upon the midnight high,
Till my weapons fell in tremor and a darkness dimmed my eye!

Hastening with a nameless terror soon I reached Sarayu's shore,
Saw a boy with hermit's tresses, and his pitcher lay before,

Weltering in a pool of red blood, lying on a gory bed,
Feebly raised his voice the hermit, and in dying accents said :

'What offence, O mighty monarch, all-unknowing have I done,
That with quick and kingly justice slayest thus a hermit's son ?

Old and feeble are my parents, sightless by the will of fate,
Thirsty in their humble cottage for their duteous boy they wait,

And thy shaft that kills me, monarch, bids my ancient parents die,
Helpless, friendless, they will perish, in their anguish deep and high !

Sacred lore and life-long penance change not mortal's earthly state,
Wherefore else they sit unconscious when their son is doomed by fate,

Or if conscious of my danger, could they dying breath recall,
Can the tall tree save the sapling doomed by woodman's axe to fall ?

Hasten to my parents, monarch, soothe their sorrow and their ire,
For the tears of good and righteous wither like the forest fire,

Short the pathway to the *asram*, soon the cottage thou shalt see,
Soothe their anger by entreaty, ask their grace and pardon free !

But before thou goest, monarch, take, O take thy torturing dart,
For it rankles in my bosom with a cruel burning smart,

And it eats into my young life as the river's rolling side,
By the rains of summer swollen eats into its yielding side.'

Writhing in his pain and anguish thus the wounded hermit cried,
And I drew the fatal arrow, and the holy hermit died !

Darkly fell the thickening shadows, stars their feeble radiance lent,
As I filled the hermit's pitcher, to his sightless parents went.

Darkly fell the moonless midnight, deeper gloom my bosom rent,
As with faint and falt'ring footsteps to the hermits slow I went.

Like two birds bereft of plumage, void of strength, deprived of flight,
Were the stricken ancient hermits, friendless, helpless, void of sight,

Lisping in their feeble accents still they whispered of their child,
Of the stainless boy whose red blood Dasa-ratha's hands defiled!

And the father heard my footsteps, spake in accents soft and kind:
'Come, my son, to waiting parents, wherefore dost thou stay behind,

Sporting in the rippling water didst thou midnight's hour beguile,
But thy faint and thirsting mother anxious waits for thee the while,

Hath my heedless word or utterance caused thy boyish bosom smart,
But a feeble father's failings may not wound thy filial heart,

Help of helpless, sight of sightless, and thy parents' life and joy,
Wherefore art thou mute and voiceless, speak, my brave and beauteous boy!'

Thus the sightless father welcomed cruel slayer of his son,
And an anguish tore my bosom for the action I had done,

Scarce upon the sonless parents could I lift my aching eye,
Scarce in faint and faltering accents to the father make reply.

For a tremor shook my person and my spirit sank in dread,
Straining all my utmost prowess, thus in quavering voice I said:

'Not thy son, O holy hermit, but a Kshatra warrior born,
Dasa-ratha stands before thee by a cruel anguish torn,

For I came to slay the tusker by Sarayu's wooded brink,
Buffalo or deer of jungle stealing for his midnight drink,

And I heard a distant gurgle, some wild beast the water drunk,—
So I thought,—some jungle tusker lifting water with its trunk,

And I sent my fatal arrow on the unknown, unseen prey,
Speeding to the spot I witnessed,—there a dying hermit lay!

From his pierced and quivering bosom then the cruel dart I drew,
And he sorrowed for his parents as his spirit heavenward flew,

Thus unconscious, holy father, I have slayed thy stainless son,
Speak my penance, or in mercy pardon deed unknowing done!'

Slow and sadly by their bidding to the fatal spot I led,
Long and loud bewailed the parents by the cold unconscious dead,

And with hymns and holy water they performed the funeral rite,
Then with tears that burnt and withered, spake the hermit in his
might:

'*Sorrow for a son beloved is a father's direst woe,*
Sorrow for a son beloved, Dasa-ratha, thou shalt know!

See the parents weep and perish, grieving for a slaughtered son,
Thou shalt weep and thou shalt perish for a loved and righteous son!

Distant is the expiation,—but in fulness of the time,
Dasa-ratha's death in anguish cleanses Dasa-ratha's crime!'

Spake the old and sightless prophet; then he made the funeral pyre,
And the father and the mother perished in the lighted fire,

Years have gone and many seasons, and in fulness of the time,
Comes the fruit of pride and folly and the harvest of my crime!

Rama eldest born and dearest, Lakshman true and faithful son,
Ah! forgive a dying father and a cruel action done,

Queen Kaikeyi, thou hast heedless brought on Raghu's race this
stain,
Banished are the guiltless children and thy lord and king is slain!

Lay thy hands on mine, Kausalya, wipe thy unavailing tear,
Speak a wife's consoling accents to a dying husband's ear,

Lay thy hands on mine, Sumitra, vision falls my closing eyes,
And for brave and banished Rama wings my spirit to the skies!"

Hushed and silent passed the midnight, feebly still the monarch
sighed,
Blessed Kausalya and Sumitra, blest his banished sons, and died.

BOOK IV

RAMA-BHARATA-SAMBADA

(The Meeting of the Princes)

The scene of this Book is laid at Chitra-kuta. Bharat returning from the kingdom of the Kaikeyas heard of his father's death and his brother's exile, and refused the throne which had been reserved for him. He wandered through the woods and jungle to Chitra-kuta, and implored Rama to return to Ayodhya, and seat himself on the throne of his father. But Rama had given his word, and would not withdraw from it.

Few passages in the Epic are more impressive than Rama's wise and kindly advice to Bharat on the duties of a ruler, and his firm refusal to Bharat's passionate appeal to seat himself on the throne. Equally touching is the lament of Queen Kausalya when she meets Sita in the dress of an anchorite in the forest.

But one of the most curious passages in the whole Epic is the speech of Jabali the Sceptic, who denied heaven and a world hereafter. In ancient India as in ancient Greece there were different schools of philosophers, some of them orthodox and some of them extremely heterodox, and the greatest latitude of free thought was permitted. In Jabali, the poet depicts a free-thinker of the broadest type. He ridicules the ideas of Duty and of Future Life with a force of reasoning which a Greek sophist and philosopher could not have surpassed. But Rama answers with the fervour of a righteous, truth-loving, God-fearing man.

All persuasion was in vain, and Bharat returned to Ayodhya with Rama's sandals, and placed them on the throne, as an emblem of Rama's sovereignty during his voluntary exile. Rama himself then left Chitra-kuta and sought the deeper forest of Dandak, so that his friends and relations might not find him again during his exile. He visited the hermitage of the Saint Atri; and the ancient and venerable wife of Atri welcomed the young Sita, and robed her in rich raiments and jewels, on the eve of her departure for the unexplored wildernesses of the south.

The portions translated in this Book are the whole or the main portions of Sections xcix., c., ci., civ., cviii., cix., cxii., and cxix. of Book ii. of the original text.

1

The Meeting of the Brothers

Sorrowing for his sire departed Bharat to Ayodhya came,
But the exile of his brother stung his noble heart to flame,

Scorning sin-polluted empire, travelling with each widowed queen,
Sought through wood and trackless jungle Chitra-kuta's peaceful scene.

Royal guards and Saint Vasishtha loitered with the dames behind,
Onward pressed the eager Bharat, Rama's hermit-home to find,

Nestled in a jungle thicket, Rama's cottage rose in sight,
Thatched with leaves and twining branches, reared by Lakshman's faithful might.

Faggots hewn of gnarlèd branches blossoms culled from bush and tree,
Coats of bark and russet garments, *kusa* spread upon the lea,

Store of horns and branching antlers, fire-wood for the dewy night,—
Spake the dwelling of a hermit suited for a hermit's rite.

"May the scene," so Bharat uttered "by the righteous *rishi* told,
Markalvati's rippling waters, Chitra-kuta's summit bold,

Mark the dark and trackless forest where the untamed tuskers roam,
And the deep and hollow caverns where the wild beasts make their home,

Mark the spacious wooded uplands, wreaths of smoke obscure the sky,
Hermits feed their flaming altars for their worship pure and high.

Done our weary work and wand'ring righteous Rama here we meet,
Saint and king and honoured elder ! Bharat bows unto his feet,

Born a king of many nations, he hath forest refuge sought,
Yielded throne and mighty kingdom for a hermit's humble cot,

Honour unto righteous Rama, unto Sita true and bold,
Theirs be fair Kosala's empire, crown and sceptre, wealth and
gold !"

Stately *Sal* and feathered palm-tree on the cottage lent their shade,
Strewn upon the sacred altar was the grass of *kusa* spread,

Gaily on the walls suspended hung two bows of ample height,
And their back with gold was pencilled, bright as INDRA's bow of
might,

Cased in broad unfailing quivers arrows shone like light of day,
And like flame-tongued fiery serpents cast a dread and lurid ray,

Resting in their golden scabbards lay the swords of warriors bold,
And the targets broad and ample bossed with rings of yellow gold,

Glove and gauntlet decked the cottage safe from fear of hostile men,
As from creatures of the forest is the lion's lordly den !

Calm in silent contemplation by the altar's sacred fire,
Holy in his pious purpose though begirt by weapons dire,

Clad in deer-skin pure and peaceful, poring on the sacred flame,
In his bark and hermit's tresses like an anchorite of fame,

Lion-shouldered, mighty-armèd, but with gentle lotus eye,
Lord of wide earth ocean-girdled, but intent on penance high,

Godlike as the holy BRAHMA, on a skin of dappled deer,
Rama sat with meek-eyed Sita, faithful Lakshman loietered near !

"Is this he whom joyous nations called to fair Ayodhya's throne,
Now the friend of forest-rangers wandering in the woods alone,

Is this he who robed in purple made Ayodhya's mansions bright,
Now in jungle bark and deer-skin clad as holy anchorite,

Is this he whose wreathèd ringlets fresh and holy fragrance shed,
Now a hermit's matted tresses cluster round his royal head,

Is this he whose royal *yajnas* filled the earth with righteous fame,
Now inured to hermit's labour by the altar's sacred flame,

Is this he whose brow and forehead royal gem and jewel graced,
Heir to proud Kosala's empire, eldest, noblest, and the best!"

Thus lamented pious Bharat for his heart was anguish-rent,
As before the feet of Rama he in loving homage bent,

"*Arya!*" in his choking accents this was all that Bharat said,
"*Arya!*" spake the young Satrughna and he bent his holy head!

Rama to his loving bosom raised his brothers from his feet,
Ah, too deep is love for utterance when divided brothers meet,

Faithful Guha, brave Sumantra, bowed to Rama's righteous feet,
And a joy and mingled sadness filled the hermit's calm retreat!

II

Bharat's Entreaty and Rama's Reply

"Speak, my true my faithful Bharat," so the righteous Rama cried,
"Wherefore to this jungle dwelling hast thou from Ayodhya hied,

Speak, my fond and loving brother, if our father bade thee come,
Leaving throne and spacious empire in this wilderness to roam?

Heir and Regent of Kosala! Dost thou tend our father well,
And obey the lofty mandate from his royal lips that fell,

And the ancient Dasa-ratha, glorious still in regal might,
Doth he pass his bright life's evening in each pure and holy rite?

Doth my mother, Queen Kausalya, still for Rama wet her eye,
And the gentle Queen Sumitra for her banished Lakshman sigh,

Doth the peerless Queen Kaikeyi pass her days in duties fair,
Guard her Bharat's mighty empire, tend him with a mother's care?

Is each holy rite and homage to the Gods and Fathers done,
Is the honour due to elders rendered by each duteous son,

Do thy warriors guard thy kingdom as of yore with matchless skill,
And with counsel deep and duteous do thy min'sters serve thy will?

Rich thy fields in corn and produce fed by rivers broad and deep,
Rich thy green unending pastures with the kine and fattened sheep,

Tend the herdsman and his cattle, tend the tiller of the soil,
Watch and help with all thy bounty workmen in their peaceful toil,

For the monarch's highest duty is to serve his people's weal
And the ruler's richest glory is to labour and to heal!

Guard thy forts with sleepless caution with the engines of the war,
With the men who shoot the arrow and who drive the flying car,

Guard Kosala's royal treasure, make thy gifts of wealth and food,
Not to lords and proud retainers, but to worthy and the good!

Render justice pure and spotless as befits thy royal line,
And to save the good and guiltless, Bharat, be it ever thine,

For the tears of suffering virtue wither like the thunder levin,
And they slay our men and cattle like the wrath of righteous heaven,

Fruitful be thy lore of Veda, fruitful be each pious rite,
Be thy queen a fruitful mother, be thy empire full of might!"

Weeping, weeping, Bharat answered Dasa-ratha's eldest son,
"Dasa-ratha walks the bright sky, for his earthly task is done!

For impelled by Queen Kaikeyi to the woods he bade thee go,
And his spotless fame was clouded and his bosom sank in woe,

And my mother, late repenting, weeps her deed of deepest shame,
Weeps her wedded lord departed, and a woman's tarnished fame!

Thou alone canst wipe this insult by a deed of kindness done,—
Rule o'er Dasa-ratha's empire, Dasa-ratha's eldest son,

Weeping queens and loyal subjects supplicate thy noble grace,—
Rule o'er Raghu's ancient empire, son of Raghu's royal race!

For our ancient Law ordaineth and thy Duty makes it plain,
Eldest-born succeeds his father as the king of earth and main,

By the fair Earth loved and welcomed, Rama, be her wedded lord,
As by planet-jewelled Midnight is the radiant Moon adored!

And thy father's ancient min'sters and thy courtiers faithful still,
Wait to do thy righteous mandate and to serve thy royal will,

As a pupil, as a brother, as a slave, I seek thy grace,—
Come and rule thy father's empire, king of Raghu's royal race!"

Weeping, on the feet of Rama, Bharat placed his lowly head,
Weeping for his sire departed, tears of sorrow Rama shed,

Then he raised his loving brother with an elder's deathless love,
Sorrow wakes our deepest kindness and our holiest feelings prove!

"But I may not," answered Rama, "seek Ayodhya's ancient throne,
For a righteous father's mandate duteous son may not disown,

And I may not, gentle brother, break the word of promise given,
To a king and to a father who is now a saint in heaven!

Not on thee, nor on thy mother, rests the censure or the blame,
Faithful to his father's wishes Rama to the forest came,

For the son and duteous consort serve the father and the lord,
Higher than an empire's glory is a father's spoken word!

All inviolate is his mandate,—on Ayodhya's jewelled throne,
Or in pathless woods and jungle Rama shall his duty own,

All inviolate is the blessing by a loving mother given,
For she blessed my life in exile like a pitying saint of heaven!

Thou shalt rule the kingdom, Bharat, guard our loving people well,
Clad in wild bark and in deer-skin I shall in the forests dwell,

So spake saintly Dasa-ratha in Ayodhya's palace hall,
And a righteous father's mandate duteous son may not recall!"

III

Kausalya's Lament and Rama's Reply

Slow and sad with Saint Vasishtha, with each widowed royal dame,
Unto Rama's hermit-cottage ancient queen Kausalya came,

And she saw him clad in wild bark like a hermit stern and high,
And an anguish smote her bosom and a tear bedewed her eye.

Rama bowed unto his mother and each elder's blessings sought,
Held their feet in salutation with a holy reverence fraught,

And the queens with loving fingers, with a mother's tender care,
Swept the dust of wood and jungle from his head and bosom fair,

Lakshman too in loving homage bent before each royal dame,
And they blessed the faithful hero spotless in his righteous fame.

Lastly came the soft-eyed Sita with obeisance soft and sweet,
And with hands in meekness folded bent her tresses to their feet,

Pain and anguish smote their bosoms, round their Sita as they
prest,
As a mother clasps a daughter, clasped her in their loving breast!

Torn from royal hall and mansion, ranger of the darksome wood,
Reft of home and kith and kindred by her forest hut she stood!

"Hast thou, daughter of Videha," weeping thus Kausalya said,
"Dwelt in woods and leafy cottage and in pathless jungle strayed,

Hast thou, Rama's royal consort, lived a homeless anchorite,
Pale with rigid fast and penance, worn with toil of righteous rite?

But thy sweet face, gentle Sita, is like faded lotus dry,
And like lily parched by sunlight, lustreless thy beauteous eye,

Like the gold untimely tarnished is thy sorrow-shaded brow,
Like the moon by shadows darkened is thy form of beauty now!

And an anguish scathes my bosom like the withering forest fire,
Thus to see thee, duteous daughter, in misfortunes deep and dire,

Dark is wide Kosala's empire, dark is Raghu's royal house,
When in woods my Rama wanders and my Rama's royal spouse!"

Sweetly, gentle Sita answered, answered Rama fair and tall,
That a righteous father's mandate duteous son may not recall!

IV

Jabali's Reasoning and Rama's Reply

Jabali a learned Brahman and a Sophist skilled in word,
Questioned Faith and Law and Duty, spake to young Ayodhya's lord:

"Wherefore, Rama, idle maxims cloud thy heart and warp thy mind,
Maxims which mislead the simple and the thoughtless human kind?

Love nor friendship doth a mortal to his kith or kindred own,
Entering on this wide earth friendless, and departing all alone,

Foolishly upon the father and the mother dotes the son,
Kinship is an idle fancy,—save thyself thy kith is none!

In the wayside inn he halteth who in distant lands doth roam,
Leaves it with the dawning daylight for another transient home,

Thus on earth are kin and kindred, home and country, wealth and store,
We but meet them on our journey, leave them as we pass before!

Wherefore for a father's mandate leave thy empire and thy throne,
Pass thy days in trackless jungle sacrificing all thy own,

Wherefore to Ayodhya's city, as to longing wife's embrace,
Speed'st thou not to rule thy empire, lord of Raghu's royal race?

Dasa-ratha claims no duty, and his will is empty word,
View him as a foreign monarch, of thy realm thou art the lord,

Dasa-ratha is departed, gone where all the mortals go,
For a dead man's idle mandate wherefore lead this life of woe?

Ah! I weep for erring mortals who on erring duty bent,
Sacrifice their dear enjoyment till their barren life is spent,

Who to Gods and to the Fathers vainly still their offerings make,
Waste of food! for God nor Father doth our pious homage take!

And the food by one partaken, can it nourish other men,
Food bestowed upon a Brahman, can it serve our Fathers then?

Crafty priests have forged these maxims and with selfish objects say,—
Make thy gifts and do thy penance, leave thy worldly wealth and pray!

There is no Hereafter, Rama, vain the hope and creed of men,
Seek the pleasures of the present, spurn illusions poor and vain,

Take the course of sense and wisdom, cast all idle faith aside,
Take the kingdom Bharat offers, rule Ayodhya in thy pride!"

"Fair thy purpose," answered Rama, "false thy reason leads astray,
Tortuous wisdom brings no profit, virtue shuns the crooked way,

For the deed proclaims the hero from the man of spacious lies,
Marks the true and upright *Arya* from the scheming worldly-wise!

If assuming virtue's mantle I should seek the sinful path,
Gods who judge our secret motives curse me with their deepest wrath,

And thy counsel helps not, *rishi*, mansions of the sky to win,
And a king his subjects follow adding deeper sin to sin!

Sweep aside thy crafty reasoning, Truth is still our ancient way,
Truth sustains the earth and nations and a monarch's righteous sway,

Mighty Gods and holy sages find in Truth their haven shore,
Scorning death and dark destruction, Truth survives for evermore,

Deadlier than the serpent's venom is the venom of a lie,
From the false, than from the cobra, men with deeper terror fly,

Dearer than the food to mortals, Truth as nourishment is given,
Truth sustains the wide creation, Truth upholds the highest heaven,

Vain were gifts and sacrifices, rigid penances were vain,
Profitless the holy *Vedas* but for Truth which they sustain,

Gifts and rites and rigid penance have no aim or purpose high,
Save in Truth which rules the wide earth and the regions of the sky,

I have plighted truth and promise and my word may not unsay,
Fourteen years in pathless forests father's mandate I obey,

And I seek no spacious reasons my relinquished throne to win,
Gods nor Fathers nor the *Vedas* counsel tortuous paths of sin!

Pardon, *rishi*, still unchanging shall remain my promise given,
To my mother Queen Kaikeyi, to my father now in heaven,

Pardon, *rishi*, still in jungle we shall seek the forest fare,
Worship Gods who watch our actions, and pervade the earth and air!

Unto Agni, unto Vayu, shall my constant prayers run,
I shall live like happy Indra hundred sacrifices done,

And the deep and darksome jungle shall be Rama's royal hall,
For a righteous father's mandate duteous son may not recall!"

V

The Sandals

Tears nor sighs nor sad entreaty Rama's changeless purpose shook,
Till once more with hands conjoined Bharat to his elder spoke:

"Rama, true to royal mercy, true to duties of thy race,
Grant this favour to thy mother, to thy brother grant this grace,

Vain were my unaided efforts to protect our father's throne,
Town and hamlet, lord and tiller, turn to thee and thee alone!

Unto Rama, friends and kinsmen, chiefs and warriors, turn in pain,
And each city chief and elder, and each humble village swain,

Base thy empire strong, unshaken, on a loyal nation's will,
With thy worth and with thy valour serve thy faithful people still!"

Rama raised the prostrate Bharat to his ever-loving breast,
And in voice of tuneful *hansa* thus his gentle speech addrest:

"Trust me, Bharat, lofty virtue, strength and will to thee belong,
Thou could'st rule a world-wide empire in thy faith and purpose strong,

And our father's ancient min'sters, ever faithful, wise and deep,
They shall help thee with their counsel and thy ancient frontiers keep.

List! the Moon may lose his lustre, Himalaya lose his snow,
Heaving Ocean pass his confines surging from the caves below,

But the truth-abiding Rama will not move from promise given,
He hath spoke and will not palter, help him righteous Gods in heaven!"

Blazing like the Sun in splendour, beauteous like the Lord of Night,
Rama vowed his Vow of Duty, changeless in his holy might!

"Humble token," answered Bharat, "still I seek from Rama's hand,
Token of his love and kindness, token of his high command,

From thy feet cast forth those sandals, they shall decorate the throne,
They shall nerve my heart to duty and shall safely guard thy own,

They shall to a loyal nation absent monarch's will proclaim,
Watch the frontiers of the empire and the people's homage claim!"

Rama gave the loosened sandals as his younger humbly prayed,
Bharat bowed to them in homage and his parting purpose said:

"Not alone will banished Rama barks and matted tresses wear,
Fourteen years the crowned Bharat will in hermit's dress appear,

Henceforth Bharat dwells in palace guised as hermit of the wood,
In the sumptuous hall of feasting wild fruit is his only food,

Fourteen years shall pass in waiting, weary toil and penance dire,
Then, if Rama comes not living, Bharat dies upon the pyre !"

VI

The Hermitage of Atri

With the sandals of his elder Bharat to Ayodhya went,
Rama sought for deeper forest on his arduous duty bent,

Wandering with his wife and Laskhman slowly sought the hermitage,
Where resided saintly Atri, Vedic Bard and ancient sage.

Anasuya, wife of Atri, votaress of Gods above,
Welcomed Sita in her cottage, tended her with mother's love,

Gave her robe and holy garland, jewelled ring and chain of gold,
Heard the tale of love and sadness which the soft-eyed Sita told :

How the monarch of Videha held the plough and tilled the earth,
From the furrow made by ploughshare infant Sita sprang to birth,

How the monarch of Videha welcomed kings of worth and pride,
Rama 'midst the gathered monarchs broke the bow and won the bride,

How by Queen Kaikeyi's mandate Rama lost his father's throne,
Sita followed him in exile in the forest dark and lone !

Softly from the lips of Sita words of joy and sorrow fell,
And the pure-souled pious priestess wept to hear the tender tale,

And she kissed her on the forehead, held her on her ancient breast,
And in mother's tender accents thus her gentle thoughts exprest :

"Sweet the tale you tell me, Sita, of thy wedding and thy love,
Of the true and tender Rama, righteous as the Gods above,

And thy wifely deep devotion fills my heart with purpose high,
Stay with us my gentle daughter for the night shades gather nigh.

Hastening from each distant region feathered songsters seek their nest,
Twitter in the leafy thickets ere they seek their nightly rest,

Hastening from their pure ablutions with their pitchers smooth and fair,
In their dripping barks the hermits to their evening rites repair,

And in sacred *agni-hotra* holy anchorites engage,
And a wreath of smoke ascending marks the altar of each sage.

Now a deeper shadow mantles bush and brake and trees around,
And a thick and inky darkness falls upon the distant ground,

Midnight prowlers of the jungle steal beneath the sable shade,
But the tame deer by the altar seeks his wonted nightly bed.

Mark! how by the stars encircled sails the radiant Lord of Night,
With his train of silver glory streaming o'er the azure height,

And thy consort waits thee, Sita, but before thou leavest, fair,
Let me deck thy brow and bosom with these jewels rich and rare,

Old these eyes and grey these tresses, but a thrill of joy is mine,
Thus to see thy youth and beauty in this gorgeous garment shine!

Pleased at heart the ancient priestess clad her in apparel meet,
And the young wife glad and grateful bowed to Anasuya's feet,

Robed and jewelled, bright and beauteous, sweet-eyed Sita softly came,
Where with anxious heart awaited Rama prince of righteous fame.

With a wifely love and longing Sita met her hero bold,
Anasuya's love and kindness in her grateful accents told,

Rama and his brother listened of the grace by Sita gained,
Favours of the ancient priestess, pious blessings she had rained.

In the *rishi's* peaceful *asram* Rama passed the sacred night,
In the hushed and silent forest silvered by the moon's pale light,

Daylight dawned, to deeper forests Rama went serene and proud,
As the sun in mid-day splendour sinks within a bank of cloud!

BOOK V

PANCHAVATI

(On the Banks of the Godavari)

The wanderings of Rama in the Deccan, his meeting with Saint Agastya, and his residence on the banks of the Godavari river, are narrated in this Book. The reader has now left Northern India and crossed the Vindhya mountains; and the scene of the present and succeeding five Books is laid in the Deccan and Southern India. The name of Agastya is connected with the Deccan, and many are the legends told of this great Saint, before whom the Vindhya mountains bent in awe, and by whose might the Southern ocean was drained. It is likely that some religious teacher of that name first penetrated beyond the Vindhyas, and founded the first Aryan settlement in the Deccan, three thousand years ago. He was pioneer, discoverer and settler,—the Indian Columbus who opened out Southern India to Aryan colonization and Aryan religion.

Two *yojanas* from Agastya's hermitage, Rama built his forest dwelling in the woods of Panchavati, near the sources of the Godavari river, and within a hundred miles from the modern city of Bombay. There he lived with his wife and brother in peace and piety, and the Book closes with the description of an Indian winter morning, when the brothers and Sita went for their ablutions to the Godavari, and thought of their distant home in Oudh. The description of the peaceful forest-life of the exiles comes in most appropriately on the eve of stirring events which immediately succeed, and which give a new turn to the story of the Epic. We now stand therefore at the turning point of the poet's narrative; he has sung of domestic incidents and of peaceful hermitage so far; he sings of dissensions and wars hereafter.

The portions translated in this Book form Sections i., xii., xiii., xv., and xvi., of Book iii. of the original text.

I

The Hermitage of Agastya

Righteous Rama, soft-eyed Sita, and the gallant Lakshman stood,
In the wilderness of Dandak,—trackless, pathless, boundless wood,

But within its gloomy gorges, dark and deep and known to few,
Humble homes of hermit sages rose before the princes' view.

Coats of bark and scattered *kusa* spake their peaceful pure abode,
Seat of pious rite and penance which with holy splendour glowed,

Forest songsters knew the *asram* and the wild deer cropt its blade,
And the sweet-voiced sylvan wood-nymph haunted oft its holy
shade,

Brightly blazed the sacred altar, vase and ladle stood around,
Fruit and blossom, skin and faggot, sanctified the holy ground.

From the broad and bending branches ripening fruits in clusters
hung,
And with gifts and rich libations hermits raised the ancient song,

Lotus and the virgin lily danced upon the rippling rill,
And the golden sunlight glittered on the greenwoods calm and still,

And the consecrated woodland by the holy hermits trod,
Shone like Brahma's sky in lustre, hallowed by the grace of God!

Rama loosened there his bow-string and the peaceful scene surveyed,
And the holy sages welcomed wanderers in the forest shade,

Rama bright as Lord of Midnight, Sita with her saintly face,
Lakshman young and true and valiant, decked with warrior's
peerless grace!

Leafy hut the holy sages to the royal guests assigned,
Brought them fruit and forest blossoms, blessed them with their
blessings kind,

"Raghu's son," thus spake the sages, "helper of each holy rite,
Portion of the royal Indra, fount of justice and of might,

On thy throne or in the forest, king of nations, lord of men,
Grant to us thy kind protection in this hermit's lonely den!"

Homely fare and jungle produce were before the princes laid,
And the toil-worn, tender Sita slumbered in the *asram's* shade.

Thus from grove to grove they wandered, to each haunt of holy sage,
Sarabhanga's sacred dwelling and Sutikshna's hermitage,

Till they met the Saint Agastya, mightiest Saint of olden time,
Harbinger of holy culture in the wilds of Southern clime!

"Eldest born of Dasa-ratha, long and far hath Rama strayed,"—
Thus to pupil of Agastya young and gallant Laskhman said,—

"With his faithful consort Sita in these wilds he wanders still,
I am righteous Rama's younger, duteous to his royal will,

And we pass these years of exile to our father's mandate true,
Fain to mighty Saint Agastya we would render homage due!"

Listening to his words the hermit sought the shrine of Sacred Fire,
Spake the message of the princes to the Saint and ancient Sire:

"Righteous Rama, valiant Lakshman, saintly Sita seek this shade,
And to see thee, radiant *rishi*, have in humble accents prayed."

"Hath he come," so spake Agastya, "Rama prince of Raghu's race,
Youth for whom this heart hath thirsted, youth endued with righteous grace,

Hath he come with wife and brother to accept our greetings kind,
Wherefore came ye for permission, wherefore linger they behind?"

Rama and the soft-eyed Sita were with gallant Lakshman led,
Where the dun deer free and fearless roamed within the holy shade,

Where the shrines of great Immortals stood in order thick and close,
And by bright and blazing altars chanted songs and hymns arose.

BRAHMA and the flaming AGNI, VISHNU lord of heavenly light,
INDRA and benign VIVASAT ruler of the azure height,

SOMA and the radiant BHAGA, and KUVERA lord of gold,
And VIDHATRI great Creator worshipped by the saints of old,

VAYU breath of living creatures, YAMA monarch of the dead,
And VARUNA with his fetters which the trembling sinners dread,

Holy Spirit of GAYATRI goddess of the morning prayer,
VASUS and the hooded NAGAS, golden-winged GARUDA fair,

KARTIKEYA heavenly leader strong to conquer and to bless,
DHARMA god of human duty and of human righteousness,

Shrines of all these bright Immortals ruling in the skies above,
Filled the pure and peaceful forest with a calm and holy love!

Girt by hermits righteous-hearted then the Saint Agastya came,
Rich in wealth of pious penance, rich in learning and in fame,

Mighty-armèd Rama marked him radiant like the midday sun,
Bowed and rendered due obeisance with each act of homage done,

Valiant Lakshman tall and stately to the great Agastya bent,
With a woman's soft devotion Sita bowed unto the saint.

Saint Agastya raised the princes, greeted them in accents sweet,
Gave them fruit and herb and water, offered them the honoured seat,

With libations unto AGNI offered welcome to each guest,
Food and drink beseeming hermits on the wearied princes pressed.

"False the hermits," spake Agastya, "who to guests their dues deny,
Hunger they in life hereafter—like the speaker of a lie,

And a royal guest and wanderer doth our foremost honour claim,
Car-borne kings protect the wide earth by their prowess and their fame,

By these fruits and forest blossoms be our humble homage shewn,
By some gift, of Rama worthy, be Agastya's blessings known!

Take this bow, heroic Rama,—need for warlike arms is thine,—
Gems of more than earthly radiance on the goodly weapon shine,

Worshipper of righteous VISHNU! VISHNU's wondrous weapon take,
Heavenly artist VISWA-KARMAN shaped this bow of heavenly make!

Take this shining dart of BRAHMA radiant like a tongue of flame,
Sped by good and worthy archer never shall it miss its aim,

And this INDRA's ample quiver filled with arrows true and keen,
Filled with arrows still unfailing in the battle's dreadful scene!

Take this sabre golden-hilted in its case of burnished gold,
Not unworthy of a monarch and a warrior true and bold,

Impious foes of bright Immortals know these weapons dread and dire,
Mowing down the ranks of foemen, scathing like the forest fire!

Be these weapons thy companions,—Rama, thou shalt need them oft,—
Meet and conquer still thy foemen like the Thunder-God aloft!"

II

THE COUNSEL OF AGASTYA

"Pleased am I," so spake Agastya, "in these forests dark and wild,
Thou hast come to seek me, Rama, with the saintly Janak's child,

But like pale and drooping blossom severed from the parent tree,
Far from home in toil and trouble, faithful Sita follows thee,

True to wedded lord and husband she hath followed Raghu's son,
With a woman's deep devotion woman's duty she hath done!

How unlike the fickle woman, true while Fame and Fortune smile,
Faithless when misfortunes gather, loveless in her wicked wile,

How unlike the changeful woman, false as light the lightnings fling,
Keen as sabre, quick as tempest, swift as bird upon its wing!

Dead to Fortune's frown or favour, Sita still in truth abides,
As the star of Arundhati in her mansion still resides,

Rest thee with thy gentle consort, farther still she may not roam,
Holier were this hermit's forest as the saintly Sita's home !"

"Great Agastya !" answered Rama, "blessed is my banished-life,
For thy kindness to an exile and his friendless homeless wife,

But in wilder, gloomier forests lonesome we must wander still,
Where a deeper, darker shadow settles on the rock and rill."

"Be it so," Agastya answered, "two short *yojans* from this place,
Wild is Panchavati's forest where unseen the wild deer race,

Godavari's limpid waters through its gloomy gorges flow,
Fruit and root and luscious berries on its silent margin grow,

Seek that spot and with thy brother build a lonesome leafy home,
Tend thy true and toil-worn Sita, farther still she may not roam !

Not unknown to me the mandate by thy royal father given,
Not unseen thy endless wanderings destined by the will of Heaven,

Therefore Panchavati's forest marked I for thy woodland stay,
Where the ripening wild fruit clusters and the wild bird trills his lay,

Tend thy dear devoted Sita and protect each pious rite,
Matchless in thy warlike weapons peerless in thy princely might !

Mark yon gloomy *Mahua* forest stretching o'er the boundless lea,
Pass that wood and turning northward seek an old *Nyagrodha* tree,

Then ascend a sloping upland by a steep and lofty hill,
Thou shalt enter Panchavati, blossom-covered, calm and still !"

Bowing to the great Agastya, Rama left the mighty sage,
Bowing to each saint and hermit, Lakshman left the hermitage,

And the princes tall and stately marched where Panchavati lay,
Soft-eyed Sita followed meekly where her Rama led the way !

III

THE FOREST OF PANCHAVATI

Godavari's limpid waters in her gloomy gorges strayed,
Unseen rangers of the jungle nestled in the darksome shade !

"Mark the woodlands," uttered Rama, "by the Saint Agastya told,
Panchavati's lonesome forest with its blossoms red and gold,

Skilled to scan the wood and jungle, Lakshman, cast thy eye around,
For our humble home and dwelling seek a low and level ground,

Where the river laves its margin with a soft and gentle kiss,
Where my sweet and soft-eyed Sita may repose in sylvan bliss,

Where the lawn is fresh and verdant and the *kusa* young and bright,
And the creeper yields her blossoms for our sacrificial rite."

"Little can I help thee, brother," did the duteous Lakshman say,
"Thou art prompt to judge and fathom, Lakshman listens to obey!"

"Mark this spot," so answered Rama, leading Lakshman by the hand,
"Soft the lawn of verdant *kusa*, beauteous blossoms light the land,

Mark the smiling lake of lotus gleaming with a radiance fair,
Wafting fresh and gentle fragrance o'er the rich and laden air,

Mark each scented shrub and creeper bending o'er the lucid wave,
Where the bank with soft caresses Godavari's waters lave!

Tuneful ducks frequent this margin, *Chakravakas* breathe of love,
And the timid deer of jungle browse within the shady grove,

And the valleys are resonant with the peacock's clarion cry,
And the trees with budding blossoms glitter on the mountains high,

And the rocks in well-marked strata in their glittering lines appear,
Like the streaks of white and crimson painted on our tuskers fair!

Stately *Sal* and feathered palm-tree guard this darksome forest-land,
Golden date and flowering mango stretch afar on either hand,

Asok thrives and blazing *Kinsuk*, *Chandan* wafts a fragrance rare,
Aswa-karna and *Khadira* by the *Sami* dark and fair,

Beauteous spot for hermit-dwelling joyous with the voice of song,
Haunted by the timid wild deer and by black buck fleet and strong!"

Foe-compelling faithful Lakshman heard the words his elder said,
And by sturdy toil and labour stately home and dwelling made,

Spacious was the leafy cottage walled with moistened earth and soft,
Pillared with the stately bamboo holding high the roof aloft,

Interlacing twigs and branches, corded from the ridge to eaves,
Held the thatch of reed and branches and of jungle grass and leaves,

And the floor was pressed and levelled and the toilsome task was
done,
And the structure rose in beauty for the righteous Raghu's son!

To the river for ablutions Lakshman went of warlike fame,
With a store of fragrant lotus and of luscious berries came,

Sacrificing to the Bright Gods sacred hymns and *mantras* said,
Proudly then unto his elder shewed the home his hand had made.

In her soft and grateful accents gentle Sita praised his skill,
Praised a brother's loving labour, praised a hero's dauntless will,

Rama clasped his faithful Lakshman in a brother's fond embrace,
Spake in sweet and kindly accents with an elder's loving grace.

"How can Rama, homeless wand'rer, priceless love like thine requite,
Let him hold thee in his bosom, soul of love and arm of might,

And our father good and gracious, in a righteous son like thee,
Lives again and treads the bright earth, from the bonds of YAMA
free!"

Thus spake Rama, and with Lakshman and with Sita child of love,
Dwelt in Panchavati's cottage as the Bright Gods dwell above!

IV

WINTER IN PANCHAVATI

Came and passed the golden autumn in the forest's gloomy shade,
And the northern blasts of winter swept along the silent glade,

When the chilly night was over, once at morn the prince of fame,
For his morning's pure ablutions to the Godavari came.

Meek-eyed Sita softly followed with the pitcher in her arms,
Gallant Lakshman spake to Rama of the Indian winter's charms :

"Comes the bright and bracing winter to the royal Rama dear,
Like a bride the beauteous season doth in richest robes appear,

Frosty air and freshening zephyrs wake to life each mart and plain,
And the corn in dewdrop sparkling makes a sea of waving green,

But the village maid and matron shun the freezing river's shore,
By the fire the village elder tells the stirring tale of yore !

With the winter's ample harvest men perform each pious rite,
To the Fathers long departed, to the Gods of holy might,

With the rite of *agrayana* pious men their sins dispel,
And with gay and sweet observance songs of love the women tell,

And the monarchs bent on conquest mark the winter's cloudless
glow,
Lead their bannered cars and forces 'gainst the rival and the foe !

Southwards rolls the solar chariot, and the cold and widowed
North,
Reft of 'bridal mark' and joyance coldly sighs her sorrows forth,

Southward rolls the solar chariot, Himalaya, 'home of snow,'
True to name and appellation doth in whiter garments glow,

Southward rolls the solar chariot, cold and crisp the frosty air,
And the wood of flower dismantled doth in russet robes appear !

Star of Pushya rules December and the night with rime is hoar,
And beneath the starry welkin in the woods we sleep no more,

And the pale moon mist-enshrouded sheds a faint and feeble beam,
As the breath obscures the mirror, winter mist obscures her gleam,

Hidden by the rising vapour faint she glistens on the dale,
Like our sun-embrownéd Sita with her toil and penance pale !

Sweeping blasts from western mountains through the gorges
    whistle by,
And the *saras* and the curlew raise their shrill and piercing cry,

Boundless fields of wheat and barley are with dewdrops moist and
    wet,
And the golden rice of winter ripens like the clustering date,

Peopled marts and rural hamlets wake to life and cheerful toil,
And the peaceful happy nations prosper on their fertile soil!

Mark the sun in morning vapours—like the moon subdued and
    pale—
Brightening as the day advances piercing through the darksome
    veil,

Mark his gay and golden lustre sparkling o'er the dewy lea,
Mantling hill and field and forest, painting bush and leaf and tree,

Mark it glisten on the green grass, on each bright and bending
    blade,
Lighten up the long drawn vista, shooting through the gloomy
    glade!

Thirst-impelled the lordly tusker still avoids the freezing drink,
Wild duck and the tuneful *hansa* doubtful watch the river's brink,

From the rivers wrapped in vapour unseen cries the wild curlew,
Unseen rolls the misty streamlet o'er its sandbank soaked in dew,

And the drooping water-lily bends her head beneath the frost,
Lost her fresh and fragrant beauty and her tender petals lost!

Now my errant fancy wanders to Ayodhya's distant town,
Where in hermit's barks and tresses Bharat wears the royal crown,

Scorning regal state and splendour, spurning pleasures loved
    of yore,
Spends his winter day in penance, sleeps at night upon the floor,

Aye! perchance Sarayu's waters seeks he now, serene and brave,
As we seek, when dawns the daylight, Godavari's limpid wave!

Rich of hue, with eye of lotus, truthful, faithful, strong of mind,
For the love he bears thee, Rama, spurns each joy of baser kind,

'False he proves unto his father who is led by mother's wile,'—
Vain this ancient impious adage—Bharat spurns his mother's guile

Bharat's mother Queen Kaikeyi, Dasa-ratha's royal spouse,
Deep in craft, brought disaster on Ayodhya's royal house!"

"Speak not thus," so Rama answered, "on Kaikeyi cast no blame,
Honour still the righteous Bharat, honour still the royal dame,

Fixed in purpose and unchanging still in jungle wilds I roam,
But thy accents, gentle Lakshman, wake a longing for my home!

And my loving mem'ry lingers on each word from Bharat fell,
Sweeter than the draught of nectar, purer than the crystal well,

And my righteous purpose falters, shaken by a brother's love,
May we meet again our brother, if it please the Gods above!"

Waked by love, a silent tear-drop fell on Godavari's wave,
True once more to righteous purpose Rama's heart was calm and
brave,

Rama plunged into the river 'neath the morning's crimson beam,
Sita softly sought the waters as the lily seeks the stream,

And they prayed to Gods and Fathers with each rite and duty
done,
And they sang the ancient *mantra* to the red and rising Sun,

With her lord, in loosened tresses Sita to her cottage came,
As with RUDRA wanders UMA in Kailasa's hill of fame!

BOOK VI

SITA-HARANA

(*Sita Lost*)

We exchange the quiet life of Rama in holy hermitages for the more stirring incidents of the Epic in this Book. The love of a Raksha princess for Rama and for Lakshman is rejected with scorn, and smarting under insult and punishment she fires her brother Ravan, the king of Ceylon, with a thirst for vengeance. The dwellers of Ceylon are described in the Epic as monsters of various forms, and able to assume different shapes at will. Ravan sends Maricha in the shape of a beautiful deer to tempt away Rama and Lakshman from the cottage, and then finds his chance for stealing away the unprotected Sita.

The misfortunes of our lives, according to Indian thinkers, are but the results of our misdeeds; calamities are brought about by our sins. And thus we find in the Indian Epic, that a dark and foul suspicion against Lakshman crossed the stainless mind of Sita, and words of unmerited insult fell from her gentle lips, on the eve of the great calamity which clouded her life ever after. It was the only occasion on which the ideal woman of the Epic harboured an unjust thought or spoke an angry word; and it was followed by a tragic fate which few women on earth have suffered. To the millions of men and women in India, Sita remains to this day the ideal of female love and female devotion; her dark suspicions against Lakshman sprang out of an excess of her affection for her husband; and her tragic fate and long trial proved that undying love.

The portions translated in this Book form the whole or the main portions of Sections xvii., xviii., xliii., xlv., xlvi., xlvii., and xlix. of Book iii. of the original text.

I

SURPA-NAKHA IN LOVE

As the Moon with starry Chitra dwells in azure skies above,
In his lonesome leafy cottage Rama dwelt in Sita's love,

And with Lakshman strong and valiant, quick to labour and obey,
Tales of bygone times recounting Rama passed the livelong day.

And it so befell, a maiden, dweller of the darksome wood,
Led by wand'ring thought or fancy once before the cottage stood,

Surpa-nakha, Raksha maiden, sister of the Raksha lord,
Came and looked with eager longing till her soul was passion-stirred!

Looked on Rama lion-chested, mighty-armèd, lotus-eyèd,
Stately as the jungle tusker, with his crown of tresses tied,

Looked on Rama lofty-fronted, with a royal visage graced,
Like KANDARPA young and lustrous, lotus-hued and lotus-faced!

What though she a Raksha maiden, poor in beauty plain in face,
Fell her glances passion-laden on the prince of peerless grace,

What though wild her eyes and tresses, and her accents counselled fear,
Soft-eyed Rama fired her bosom, and his sweet voice thrilled her ear,

What though bent on deeds unholy, holy Rama won her heart,
And for love makes bold a female, thus did she her thoughts impart:

"Who be thou in hermit's vestments, in thy native beauty bright,
Friended by a youthful woman, armèd with thy bow of might,

Who be thou in these lone regions where the Rakshas hold their sway,
Wherefore in a lonely cottage in this darksome jungle stay?"

With his wonted truth and candour Rama spake sedate and bold,
And the story of his exile to the Raksha maiden told:

"Dasa-ratha of Ayodhya ruled with INDRA's godlike fame,
And his eldest, first born Rama, by his mandate here I came,

Younger Lakshman strong and valiant doth with me these forests roam,
And my wife, Videha's daughter, Sita makes with me her home.

Duteous to my father's bidding, duteous to my mother's will,
Striving in the cause of virtue in the woods we wander still,

Tell me, female of the forest, who thou be and whence thy birth,
Much I fear thou art a Raksha wearing various forms on earth!"

"Listen," so spake Surpa-nakha, "if my purpose thou wouldst know,
I am Raksha, Surpa-nakha, wearing various shapes below,

Know my brothers, royal Ravan, Lanka's lord from days of old,
Kumbha-karna dread and dauntless, and Bibhishan true and bold,

Khara and the doughty Dushan with me in these forests stray,
But by Rama's love emboldened I have left them on the way!

Broad and boundless is my empire and I wander in my pride,
Thee I choose as lord and husband,—cast thy human wife aside,

Pale is Sita and mis-shapen, scarce a warrior's worthy wife,
To a nobler, lordlier female consecrate thy gallant life!

Human flesh is food of Rakshas! weakling Sita I will slay,
Slay that boy thy stripling brother,—thee as husband I obey,

On the peaks of lofty mountains, in the forests dark and lone,
We shall range the boundless woodlands and the joys of dalliance prove!"

II

SURPA-NAKHA PUNISHED

Rama heard her impious purpose and a gentle smile repressed,
To the foul and forward female thus his mocking words addressed,

"List, O passion-smitten maiden! Sita is my honoured wife,
With a rival loved and cherished cruel were thy wedded life!

But no consort follows Lakshman, peerless is his comely face,
Dauntless is his warlike valour, matchless is his courtly grace,

And he leads no wife or consort to this darksome woodland grove,
With no rival to thy passion seek his ample-hearted love!"

Surpa-nakha passion-laden then on Lakshman turned her eye,
But in merry mocking accents smiling Lakshman made reply:

"Ruddy in thy youthful beauty like the lotus in her pride,
I am slave of royal Rama, would'st thou be a vassal's bride?

Rather be his younger consort, banish Sita from his arms,
Spurning Sita's faded beauty let him seek thy fresher charms,

Spurning Sita's faded graces let him brighter pleasures prove,
Wearied with a woman's dalliance let him court a Raksha's love!"

Wrath of unrequited passion raged like madness in her breast,
Torn by anger strong as tempest thus her answer she addrest:

"Are these mocking accents uttered, Rama, to insult my flame,
Feasting on her faded beauty dost thou still revere thy dame?

But beware a Raksha's fury and an injured female's wrath,
Surpa-nakha slays thy consort, bears no rival in her path!"

Fawn-eyed Sita fell in terror as the Raskha rose to slay,
So beneath the flaming meteor sinks Rohini's softer ray,

And like Demon of Destruction furious, Surpa-nakha came,
Rama rose to stop the slaughter and protect his helpless dame.

"Brother, we have acted wrongly, for with those of savage breed,
Word in jest is courting danger,—this the penance of our deed,

Death perchance or death-like stupor hovers o'er my loved dame,
Let me wake to life my Sita, chase this female void of shame!"

Lakshman's anger leaped like lightning as the female hovered near,
With his sword the wrathful warrior cleft her nose and either ear,

Surpa-nakha in her anguish raised her accents shrill and high,
And the rocks and wooded valleys answered back the dismal cry,

Khara and the doughty Dushan heard the far-resounding wail,
Saw her red disfigured visage, heard her sad and woeful tale !

III

Rama's Departure

Vainly fought the vengeful Khara, doughty Dushan vainly bled,
Rama and the valiant Lakshman strewed the forest with the dead,

Till the humbled Surpa-nakha to her royal brother hied,
Spake her sorrows unto Ravan and Maricha true and tried.

Shape of deer unmatched in beauty now the deep Maricha wore,
Golden tints upon his haunches, sapphire on his antlers bore,

Till the woodland-wand'ring Sita marked the creature in his pride,
Golden was his neck of beauty, silver white his flank and side !

"Come, my lord and gallant Lakshman," thus the raptur'd Sita spake,
"Mark the deer of wondrous radiance browsing by the forest brake !"

"Much my heart misgives me, sister," Lakshman hesitated still,
"'Tis some deep deceitful Raksha wearing every shape at will,

Monarchs wand'ring in this forest, hunting in this lonely glen,
Oft waylaid by artful Rakshas are by deep devices slain,

Bright as day-god or *Gandharva*, woodland scenes they love to stray,
Till they fall upon the heedless, quick to slaughter and to slay,

Trust me, not in jewelled lustre forest creatures haunt the green,
'Tis some *maya* and illusion, trust not what thy eyes have seen !"

Vainly spake the watchful Lakshman in the arts of Rakshas skilled,
For with forceful fascination Sita's inmost heart was thrilled,

"Husband, good and ever gracious," sweetly thus implored the wife,
"I would tend this thing of beauty,—sharer of my forest life !

I have witnessed in this jungle graceful creatures passing fair,
Chowri and the gentle roebuck, antelope of beauty rare,

I have seen the lithesome monkey sporting in the branches' shade,
Grizzly bear that feeds on *Mahua*, and the deer that crops the blade,

I have marked the stately wild bull dash into the deepest wood,
And the *Kinnar* strange and wondrous as in sylvan wilds he stood,

But these eyes have never rested on a form so wondrous fair,
On a shape so full of beauty, decked with tints so rich and rare!

Bright his bosom gem-bespangled, soft the lustre of his eye,
Lighting up the gloomy jungle as the Moon lights up the sky,

And his gentle voice and glances and his graceful steps and light,
Fill my heart with eager longing and my soul with soft delight!

If alive that beauteous object thou canst capture in thy way,
As thy Sita's sweet companion in these woodlands he will stay,

And when done our days of exile, to Ayodhya will repair,
Dwell in Sita's palace chamber nursed by Sita's tender care,

And our royal brother Bharat oft will praise his strength and speed,
And the queens and royal mothers pause the gentle thing to feed!

If alive this wary creature be it, husband, hard to take,
Slay him and his skin of lustre cherish for thy Sita's sake,

I will as a golden carpet spread the skin upon the grass,
Sweet memento of this forest when our forest days will pass!

Pardon if an eager longing which befits a woman ill,
And an unknown fascination doth my inmost bosom fill,

As I mark his skin bespangled and his antlers' sapphire ray,
And his coat of starry radiance glowing in the light of day!"

Rama bade the faithful Lakshman with the gentle Sita stay,
Long through woods and gloomy gorges vainly held his cautious way,

Vainly set the snare in silence by the lake and in the dale,
'Scaping every trap, Maricha, pierced by Rama's arrows fell,

Imitating Rama's accents uttered forth his dying cry:
"Speed, my faithful brother Lakshman, helpless in the woods I die!"

IV

Lakshman's Departure

"Heardst that distant cry of danger?" questioned Sita in distress,
"Woe, to me! who in my frenzy sent my lord to wilderness,

Speed, brave Lakshman, help my Rama, doleful was his distant cry,
And my fainting bosom falters and a dimness clouds my eye!

To the dread and darksome forest with thy keenest arrows speed,
Help thy elder and thy monarch, sore his danger and his need,

For perchance the cruel Rakshas gather round his lonesome path,
As the mighty bull is slaughtered by the lions in their wrath!"

Spake the hero: "Fear not, Sita! Dwellers of the azure height,
Rakshas nor the jungle-rangers match the peerless Rama's might,

Rama knows no dread or danger, and his mandate still I own,
And I may not leave thee, Lady, in this cottage all alone!

Cast aside thy causeless terror; in the sky or earth below,
In the nether regions, Rama knows no peer or equal foe,

He shall slay the deer of jungle, he shall voice no dastard cry,
'Tis some trick of wily Rakshas in this forest dark and high!

Sita, thou hast heard my elder bid me in this cottage stay,
Lakshman may not leave thee, Lady, for his duty—to obey,

Ruthless Rakshas roam the forest to revenge their leader slain,
Various are their arts and accents; chase thy thought of causeless
pain!"

Sparkled Sita's eye in anger, frenzy marked her speech and word,
For a woman's sense is clouded by the danger of her lord:

"Markest thou my Rama's danger with a cold and callous heart,
Courtest thou the death of elder in thy deep deceitful art,

In thy semblance of compassion dost thou hide a cruel craft,
As in friendly guise the foeman hides his death-compelling shaft,

Following like a faithful younger in this dread and lonesome land,
Seekest thou the death of elder to enforce his widow's hand?

False thy hope as foul thy purpose! Sita is a faithful wife,
Sita follows saintly Rama, true in death as true in life!"

Quivered Lakshman's frame in anguish and the tear stood in his eye,
Fixed in faith and pure in purpose, calm and bold he made reply:

"Unto me a queen and Goddess,—as a mother to a son,—
Answer to thy heedless censure patient Lakshman speaketh none,

Daughter of Videha's monarch,—pardon if I do thee wrong,—
Fickle is the faith of woman, poison-dealing is her tongue!

And thy censure, trust me, Lady, scathes me like a burning dart,
Free from guile is Lakshman's purpose, free from sin is Lakshman's heart,

Witness ye my truth of purpose, unseen dwellers of the wood,
Witness, I for Sita's safety by my elder's mandate stood,

Duteous to my queen and elder, I have toiled and worked in vain,
Dark suspicion and dishonour cast on me a needless stain!

Lady! I obey thy mandate, to my elder now I go,
Guardian Spirits of the forest watch thee from each secret foe,

Omens dark and signs of danger meet my pained and aching sight,
May I see thee by thy Rama, guarded by his conquering might!"

V

Ravan's Coming

Ravan watched the happy moment burning with a vengeful spite,
Came to sad and sorrowing Sita in the guise of anchorite,

Tufted hair and russet garment, sandals on his feet he wore,
And depending from his shoulders on a staff his vessel bore.

And he came to lonely Sita, for each warlike chief was gone,
As the darkness comes to evening lightless from the parted Sun,

And he cast his eyes on Sita, as a *graha* casts its shade
On the beauteous star Rohini when the bright Moon's glories fade,

Quaking Nature knew the moment; silent stood the forest trees,
Conscious of a deed of darkness fell the fragrant forest breeze,

Godavari's troubled waters trembled 'neath his lurid glance,
And his red eye's fiery lustre sparkled in the wavelets' dance!

Mute and still were forest creatures when in guise of anchorite,
Unto Sita's lonely cottage pressed the Raksha in his might,

Mute and voiceless was the jungle as he cast on her his eye,
As across the star of Chitra, planet Sani walks the sky!

Ravan stood in hermit's vestments,—vengeful purpose unrevealed,
As a deep and darksome cavern is by grass and leaf concealed,

Ravan stood sedate and silent, and he gazed on Rama's queen,
Ivory brow and lip of coral, sparkling teeth of pearly sheen!

Lighting up the lonely cottage Sita sat in radiance high,
As the Moon with streaks of silver fills the lonely midnight sky,

Lighting up the gloomy woodlands with her eyes serenely fair,
With her bark-clad shape of beauty mantled by her raven hair!

Ravan fired by impure passion fixed on her his lustful eye,
And the light that lit his glances gave his holy texts the lie,

Ravan in his flattering accents, with a soft and soothing art,
Praised the woman's peerless beauty to subdue the woman's heart:

"Beaming in thy golden beauty, robed in sylvan russet dress,
Wearing wreath of fragrant lotus like a nymph of wilderness,

Art thou *Sri* or radiant *Gauri*, maid of Fortune or of Fame,
Nymph of Love or sweet Fruition, what may be thy sacred name?

On thy lips of ruddy coral teeth of tender jasmine shine,
In thy eyes of limpid lustre dwells a light of love divine,

Tall and slender, softly rounded, are thy limbs of beauty rare,
Like the swelling fruit of *tala* heaves thy bosom sweetly fair!

Smiling lips that tempt and ravish, lustre that thy dark eyes beam,
Crush my heart, as rolling waters crush the margin of the stream,

And thy wealth of waving tresses mantles o'er thy budding charms,
And thy waist of slender beauty courts a lover's circling arms!

Goddess or *Gandharva* maiden wears no brighter form or face,
Woman seen by eyes of mortals owns not such transcendent grace,

Wherefore then, in lonesome forest, nymph or maiden, make thy
stay,
Where the jungle creatures wander and the Rakshas hold their
sway?

Royal halls and stately mansions were for thee a meeter home,
And thy steps should grace a palace, not in pathless forest roam,

Blossoms rich, not thorn of jungle, decorate a lady's bower,
Silken robes, not sylvan garments, heighten Beauty's potent
power!

Lady of the sylvan forest! other destiny is thine,—
As a bride beloved and courted in thy bridal garments shine,

Choose a loved and lordly suitor who shall wait on thee in pride,
Choose a hero worth thy beauty, be a monarch's queenly bride!

Speak thy lineage, heaven-descended! who may be thy parents
high,
Rudras or the radiant *Maruts*, *Vasus* leaders of the sky,

All unworthy is this forest for a nymph or heavenly maid,
Beasts of prey infest the jungle, Rakshas haunt its gloomy shade,

Lions dwell in lonely caverns, tuskers ford the silent lake,
Monkeys sport on pendant branches, tigers steal beneath the brake,

Wherefore then this dismal forest doth thy fairy face adorn,
Who art thou and whence descended, nymph or maid or goddess-
born?"

VI

Ravan's Wooing

"Listen, Brahman!" answered Sita,—unsuspecting in her mind,
That she saw a base betrayer in a hermit seeming kind,—

"I am born of royal Janak, ruler of Videha's land,
Rama prince of proud Kosala by his valour won my hand.

Years we passed in peaceful pleasure in Ayodhya's happy clime,
Rich in every rare enjoyment gladsome passed our happy time,

Till the monarch Dasa-ratha,—for his days were almost done,—
Wished to crown the royal Rama as his Heir and Regent son.

But the scheming Queen Kaikeyi claimed a long-forgotten boon,
That my consort should be exiled and her son should fill the throne,

She would take no rest or slumber, nourishment of drink or food,
Till her Bharat ruled the empire, Rama banished to the wood!

Five and twenty righteous summers graced my good and gracious lord,
True to faith and true to duty, true in purpose deed and word,

Loved of all his loyal people, rich in valour and in fame,
For the rite of consecration Rama to his father came.

Spake Kaikeyi to my husband:—'List thy father's promise fair,
Bharat shall be ruling monarch, do thou to the woods repair,'—

Ever gentle, ever duteous, Rama listened to obey,
And through woods and pathless jungles we have held our lonely way!

This, O pious-hearted hermit, is his story of distress,
And his young and faithful brother follows him in wilderness,

Lion in his warlike valour, hermit in his saintly vow,
Lakshman with his honoured elder wanders through the forest now.

Rest thee here, O holy Brahman, rich in piety and fame,
Till the forest-ranging brothers greet thee with the forest game,

Speak, if so it please thee, father, what great *rishi* claims thy birth,
Wherefore in this pathless jungle wand'rest friendless on this earth."

"Brahman nor a righteous *rishi*," royal Ravan made reply,
"Leader of the wrathful Rakshas, Lanka's lord and king am I,

He whose valour quells the wide-world, Gods above and men below,
He whose proud and peerless prowess Rakshas and Asuras know!

But thy beauty's golden lustre, Sita, wins my royal heart,
Be a sharer of my empire, of my glory take a part,

Many queens of queenly beauty on the royal Ravan wait,
Thou shalt be their reigning empress, thou shalt own my regal state!

Lanka girt by boundless ocean is of royal towns the best,
Seated in her pride and glory on a mountain's towering crest,

And in mountain paths and woodlands thou shalt with thy Ravan stray,
Not in Godavari's gorges through the dark and dreary day,

And five thousand gay-dressed damsels shall upon my Sita wait,
Queen of Ravan's true affection, proud partaker of his state!"

Sparkled Sita's eyes in anger and a tremor shook her frame,
As in proud and scornful accents answered thus the royal dame:

"Knowest thou Rama great and godlike, peerless hero in the strife,
Deep, uncompassed, like the ocean?—I am Rama's wedded wife!

Knowest thou Rama proud and princely, sinless in his saintly life,
Stately as the tall *Nyagrodha*?—I am Rama's wedded wife!

Mighty-armed, mighty-chested, mighty with his bow and sword,
Lion midst the sons of mortals,—Rama is my wedded lord!

Stainless as the Moon in glory, stainless in his deed and word,
Rich in valour and in virtue,—Rama is my wedded lord!

Sure thy fitful life is shadowed by a dark and dreadful fate,
Since in frenzy of thy passion courtest thou a warrior's mate,

Tear the tooth of hungry lion while upon the calf he feeds,
Touch the fang of deadly cobra while his dying victim bleeds,

Aye uproot the solid mountain from its base of rocky land,
Ere thou win the wife of Rama stout of heart and strong of hand!

Pierce thy eye with point of needle till it racks thy tortured head,
Press thy red tongue cleft and bleeding on the razor's shining
blade,

Hurl thyself upon the ocean from a towering peak and high,
Snatch the orbs of day and midnight from their spheres in azure
sky,

Tongues of flaming conflagration in thy flowing dress enfold,
Ere thou take the wife of Rama to thy distant dungeon hold,

Ere thou seek to insult Rama unrelenting in his wrath,
O'er a bed of pikes of iron tread a softer easier path!"

VII

RAVAN'S TRIUMPH

Vain her threat and soft entreaty, Ravan held her in his wrath,
As the planet Budha captures fair Rohini in his path,

By his left hand tremor-shaken, Ravan held her streaming hair,
By his right the ruthless Raksha lifted up the fainting fair!

Unseen dwellers of the woodlands watched the dismal deed of
shame,
Marked the mighty-armed Raksha lift the poor and helpless dame,

Seat her on his car celestial yoked with asses winged with speed,
Golden in its shape and radiance, fleet as INDRA's heavenly steed?

Angry threat and sweet entreaty Ravan to her ears addressed,
As the struggling fainting woman still he held upon his breast,

Vain his threat and vain entreaty, "Rama! Rama!" still she cried,
To the dark and distant forest where her noble lord had hied.

Then arose the car celestial o'er the hill and wooded vale,
Like a snake in eagle's talons Sita writhed with piteous wail,

Dim and dizzy, faint and faltering, still she sent her piercing cry,
Echoing through the boundless woodlands, pealing to the upper sky:

"Save me, mighty-armed Lakshman, stainless in thy heart and deed,
Save a faithful wife and woman from a Raksha's lust and greed,

True and faithful was thy warning,—false and foul the charge I made,
Pardon, friend, an erring sister, pardon words a woman said!

Help me, ever righteous Rama, duty bade thee yield thy throne,
Duty bids thee smite the sinful, save the wife who is thy own,

Thou art king and stern chastiser of each deed of sin and shame,
Hurl thy vengeance on the Raksha who insults thy faithful dame!

Deed of sin, unrighteous Ravan, brings in time its dreadful meed,
As the young corn grows and ripens from the small and living seed,

For this deed of insult, Ravan, in thy heedless folly done,
Death of all thy race and kindred thou shalt reap from Raghu's son!

Darksome woods of Panchavati, Janasthana's smiling vale,
Flowering trees and winding creepers, murmur to my lord this tale,

Sweet companions of my exile, friends who cheered my woodland stay,
Speak to Rama, that his Sita ruthless Ravan bears away!

Towering peaks and lofty mountains, wooded hills sublime and high,
Far-extending gloomy ranges heaving to the azure sky,

In your voice of pealing thunder to my lord and consort say,
Speak to Rama, that his Sita ruthless Ravan bears away!

Unseen dwellers of the woodlands, spirits of the rock and fell,
Sita renders you obeisance as she speaks her sad farewell,

Whisper to my righteous Rama when he seeks his homeward way,
Speak to Rama, that his Sita ruthless Ravan bears away!

Ah, my Rama, true and tender! thou hast loved me as thy life,
From the foul and impious Raksha thou shalt still redeem thy wife,

Ah, my Rama, mighty-armèd! vengeance soon shall speed thy way,
When thou hearest, helpless Sita is by Ravan torn away!

And thou royal bird, Jatayu, witness Ravan's deed of shame,
Witness how he courts destruction, stealing Rama's faithful dame,

Rama and the gallant Lakshman soon shall find their destined prey,
When they know that trusting Sita is by Ravan torn away!"

Vainly wept the anguished Sita; vain Jatayu in his wrath,
Fought with beak and bloody talons to impede the Raksha's path,

Pierced and bleeding fell the vulture; Ravan fled with Rama's bride,
Where amidst the boundless ocean Lanka rose in towering pride!

BOOK VII

KISHKINDHA

(In the Nilgiri Mountains)

Rama's wanderings in the Nilgiri mountains, and his alliance with Sugriva, the chief of these regions, form the subject of the Book. With that contempt for aboriginal races which has marked civilized conquerors in all ages, the poet describes the dwellers of these regions as monkeys and bears. But the modern reader sees through these strange epithets; and in the description of the social and domestic manners, the arts and industries, the sacred rites and ceremonies, and the civic and political life of the Vanars, the reader will find that the poet even imports Aryan customs into his account of the dwellers of Southern India. They formed an alliance with Rama, they fought for him and triumphed with him, and they helped him to recover his wife from the king of Ceylon.

The portions translated in this Book form Sections v., xv., xvi., xxvi., a portion of Section xxviii., and an abstract of Sections xl. to xliii. of Book iv. of the original text.

I

Friends in Misfortune

Long and loud lamented Rama by his lonesome cottage door,
'Janasthana's woodlands answered, Panchavati's echoing shore,

Long he searched in wood and jungle, mountain crest and pathless plain,
Till he reached the Malya mountains stretching to the southern main.

There Sugriva king of Vanars, Hanuman his henchman brave,
Banished from their home and empire lived within the forest cave,

To the exiled king Sugriva, Hanuman his purpose told,
As he marked the pensive Rama wand'ring with his brother bold:

"Mark the sons of Dasa-ratha banished from their royal home,
Duteous to their father's mandate in these pathless forests roam,

Great was monarch Dasa-ratha famed for sacrifice divine,
Raja-suya, *Aswa-medha*, and for gift of gold and kine,

By a monarch's stainless duty people's love the monarch won,
By a woman's false contrivance banished he his eldest son!

True to duty, true to virtue, Rama passed his forest life,
Till a false perfidious Raksha stole his fair and faithful wife,

And the anguish-stricken husband seeks thy friendship and thy aid,—
Mutual sorrow blends your fortunes, be ye friends in mutual need!"

Bold Sugriva heard the counsel, and to righteous Rama hied,
And the princes of Ayodhya with his greetings gratified:

"*Well I know thee, righteous Rama, soul of piety and love,*
And thy duty to thy father and thy faith in Gods above,

Fortune favours poor Sugriva, Rama courts his humble aid,
In our deepest direst danger be our truest friendship made!

Equal is our fateful fortune,—I have lost a queenly wife,
Banished from Kishkindha's empire here I lead a forest life,

Pledge of love and true alliance, Rama, take this proffered hand,
Banded by a common sorrow we shall fall or stoutly stand!"

Rama grasped the hand he offered, and the tear was in his eye,
And they swore undying friendship o'er the altar blazing high,

Hanuman with fragrant blossoms sanctified the sacred rite,
And the comrades linked by sorrow walked around the altar's light,

And their word and troth they plighted: "In our happiness and woe,
We are friends in thought and action, we will face our common foe!"

And they broke a leafy *Sal* tree, spread it underneath their feet,
Rama and his friend Sugriva sat upon the common seat,

And a branch of scented *Chandan* with its tender blossoms graced,
Hanuman as seat of honour for the faithful Lakshman placed.

"Listen, Rama," spake Sugriva, "reft of kingdom, reft of wife,
Fleeing to these rugged mountains I endure a forest life,

For my tyrant brother Bali rules Kishkindha all alone,
Forced my wife from my embraces, drove me from my father's
throne,

Trembling in my fear and anguish I endure a life of woe,
Render me my wife and empire from my brother and my foe!"

"Not in vain they seek my succour," so the gallant Rama said,
"Who with love and offered friendship seek my counsel and my aid,

Not in vain these glistening arrows in my ample quiver shine,
Bali dies the death of tyrants, wife and empire shall be thine!

Quick as INDRA's *forkèd lightning are these arrows feather-plumed,*
Deadly as the hissing serpent are these darts with points illumed,

And this day shall not be ended ere it sees thy brother fall,
As by lurid lightning severed sinks the crest of mountain tall!"

II

The Counsel of Tara

Linked in bonds of faithful friendship Rama and Sugriva came,
Where in royal town Kishkindha, Bali ruled with warlike fame,

And a shout like troubled ocean's or like tempest's deafening roar
Spake Sugriva's mighty challenge to the victor king once more!

Bali knew that proud defiance shaking sky and solid ground,
And like sun by eclipse shaded, dark and pale he looked around,

And his teeth were set in anger and a passion lit his eye,
As a tempest stirs a torrent when its lilies scattered lie,

And he rose in wrath terrific with a thought of vengeance dread,
And the firm earth shook and trembled 'neath his proud and
haughty tread!

But the true and tender Tara held her husband and her lord,
And a woman's deeper wisdom spake in woman's loving word:

"Wherefore like a rain-fed torrent swells thy passion in its sway,
Thoughts of wrath like withered blossoms from thy bosom cast
away,

Wait till dawns another morning, wait till thou dost truly know,
With what strength and added forces comes again thy humbled foe.

Crushed in combat faint Sugriva fled in terror and in pain,
Trust me, not without a helper comes he to the fight again,

Trust me, lord, that loud defiance is no coward's falt'ring cry,
Conscious strength not hesitation speaks in voice so proud and
high!

Much my woman's heart misgives me, not without a mighty aid,
Not without a daring comrade comes Sugriva to this raid,

Not with feeble friend Sugriva seeks alliance in his need,
Nor invokes a powerless chieftain in his lust and in his greed.

Mighty is his royal comrade,—listen, husband, to my word,
What my son in forest confines from his messengers hath heard,—

Princes from Ayodhya's country peerless in the art of war,
Rama and the valiant Lakshman in these forests wander far,

Much I fear, these matchless warriors have their aid and counsel lent,
Conscious of his strength Sugriva hath this proud defiance sent!

To his foes resistless Rama is a lightning from above,
To his friends a tree of shelter, soul of tenderness and love,

Dearer than his love of glory is his love to heal and bless,
Dearer than the crown and empire is his hermit's holy dress,

Not with such, my lord and husband, seek a vain unrighteous strife,
For, like precious ores in mountains, virtues dwell in Rama's life.

Make Sugriva thy companion, make him Regent and thy Heir,
Discord with a younger brother rends an empire broad and fair,

Make thy peace with young Sugriva, nearest and thy dearest kin,
Brother's love is truest safety, brother's hate is deadliest sin!

Trust me, monarch of Kishkindha, trust thy true and faithful wife,
Thou shalt find no truer comrade than Sugriva in thy life,

Wage not then a war fraternal, smite him not in sinful pride,
As a brother and a warrior let him stand by Bali's side.

Listen to thy Tara's counsel if to thee is Tara dear,
If thy wife is true in duty scorn not Tara's wifely tear,

Not with Rama prince of virtue wage a combat dread and high,
Not with Rama prince of valour, peerless like the Lord of sky!"

III

The Fall of Bali

Star-eyed Tara softly counselled pressing to her consort's side,
Mighty Bali proudly answered with a warrior's lofty pride:

"Challenge of a humbled foeman and a younger's haughty scorn
May not, shall not, tender Tara, by a king be meekly borne!

Bali turns not from encounter even with his dying breath,
Insult from a foe, unanswered, is a deeper stain than death,

And Sugriva's quest for combat Bali never shall deny,
Though sustained by Rama's forces and by Rama's prowess high!

Free me from thy sweet embraces and amidst thy maids retire,
Woman's love and soft devotion woman's timid thoughts inspire,

Fear not, Tara, blood of brother Bali's honour shall not stain,
I will quell his proud presumption, chase him from this realm again,

Free me from thy loving dalliance, midst thy damsels seek thy place,
Till I come a happy victor to my Tara's fond embrace!"

Slow and sad with sweet obeisance Tara stepped around her lord,
Welling tear-drops choked her accents as she prayed in stifled word,

Slow and sad with swelling bosom Tara with her maids retired,
Bali issued proud and stately with the thought of vengeance fired!

Hissing like an angry cobra, city's lofty gates he past,
And his proud and angry glances fiercely all around he cast,

Till he saw the bold Sugriva, gold-complexioned, red with ire,
Girded for the dubious combat, flaming like the forest fire!

Bali braced his warlike garments and his hand he lifted high,
Bold Sugriva raised his right arm with a proud and answering cry,

Bali's eyes were red as copper and his chain was burnished gold,
To his brother bold Sugriva thus he spake in accents bold:

"Mark this iron fist, intruder, fatal is its vengeful blow,
Crushed and smitten thou shalt perish and to nether world shalt go."

"Nay that fate awaits thee, Bali," spake Sugriva armed for strife,
"When this right arm smites thy forehead, from thy bosom rends
thy life!"

Closed the chiefs in fatal combat, each resistless in his pride,
And like running rills from mountains poured their limbs the
purple tide,

Till Sugriva quick uprooting *Sal* tree from the jungle wood,
As the dark cloud hurls the lightning, hurled it where his brother
stood,

Staggering 'neath the blow terrific Bali reeled and almost fell,
As a proud ship overladen reels upon the ocean's swell!

But with fiercer rage and fury Bali in his anguish rose,
And with mutual blows they battled,—brothers and relentless foes,

Like the sun and moon in conflict or like eagles in their fight,
Still they fought with cherished hatred and an unforgotten spite,

Till with mightier force and fury Bali did his younger quell,
Faint Sugriva fiercely struggling 'neath his brother's prowess fell!

Still the wrathful rivals wrestled with their bleeding arms and knees,
With their nails like claws of tigers and with riven rocks and trees,

And as INDRA battles Vritra in the tempest's pealing roar,
Blood-stained Bali, red Sugriva, strove and struggled, fought and tore,

Till Sugriva faint and falt'ring fell like Vritra from the sky,
To his comrade and his helper turned his faint and pleading eye!

Ah! those soft and pleading glances smote the gentle Rama's heart,
On his bow of ample stature Rama raised the fatal dart,

Like the fatal disc of YAMA was his proudly circled bow,
Like a snake of deadly poison flew his arrow swift and low,

Winged dwellers of the forest heard the twang with trembling fear,
Echoing woods gave back the accent, lightly fled the startled deer,

And as INDRA's flag is lowered when the Aswin winds prevail,
Lofty Bali pierced and bleeding by that fatal arrow fell!

IV

THE CONSECRATION OF SUGRIVA

Tears of love the tender Tara on her slaughtered hero shed,
E'en Sugriva's bosom melted when he saw his brother dead,

And each Vanar chief and warrior, *maha-matra*, lord and peer,
Gathered round the sad Sugriva wet with unavailing tear!

And they girt the victor Rama and they praised his wond'rous might,
As the heavenly *rishis* gather circling BRAHMA's throne of light,

Hanuman of sun-like radiance, lofty as a hill of gold,
Clasped his hands in due obeisance, spake in accents calm and bold:

"By thy prowess, peerless Rama, prince Sugriva is our lord,
To his father's throne and empire, to his father's town restored,

Cleansed by bath and fragrant unguents and in royal garments gay,
He shall with his gold and garlands homage to the victor pay,

To the rock-bound fair Kishkindha do thy friendly footsteps bend,
And as monarch of the Vanars consecrate thy grateful friend!"

"Fourteen years," so Rama answered, "by his father's stern command,
In a city's sacred confines banished Rama may not stand,

Friend and comrade, brave Sugriva, enter thou the city wall,
And assume the royal sceptre in thy father's royal hall.

Gallant Angad, son of Bali, is in regal duties trained,
Ruling partner of thy empire be the valiant prince ordained,

Eldest son of eldest brother,—such the maxim that we own,—
Worthy of his father's kingdom, doth ascend his father's throne.

Listen! 'tis the month of *Sravan*, now begins the yearly rain,
In these months of wind and deluge thoughts of vengeful strife were vain,

Enter then thy royal city, fair Kishkindha be thy home,
With my ever faithful Lakshman let me in these mountains roam.

Spacious is yon rocky cavern fragrant with the mountain air,
Bright with lily and with lotus, watered by a streamlet fair,

Here we dwell till month of *Kartik* when the clouded sky will clear,
And the time of war and vengeance on our foeman shall be near."

Bowing to the victor's mandate brave Sugriva marched in state,
And the host of thronging Vanars entered by the city gate,

Prostrate chiefs with due obeisance rendered homage, one and all,
And Sugriva blessed his people, stepped within the palace hall.

And they sprinkled sacred water from the vases jewel-graced,
And they waved the fan of *chowri*, raised the sun-shade silver-laced,

And they spread the gold and jewel, grain and herb and fragrant *ghee*,
Sapling twigs and bending branches, blossoms from the flowering tree.

Milk-white garments gem-bespangled, and the *Chandan's* fragrant dye,
Wreaths and spices, snow-white lilies, lotus azure as the sky,

Jatarupa and *Priyangu*, honey, curd and holy oil,
Costly sandals gilt and jewelled, tiger-skin the hunter's spoil!

Decked in gold and scented garlands, robed in radiance rich and rare,
Sweetly stepped around Sugriva sixteen maidens passing fair,

Priests received the royal bounty, gift and garment gold-belaced,
And they lit the holy altar with the sacred *mantra* graced,

And they poured the sweet libation on the altar's lighted flame,
And on throne of royal splendour placed the chief of royal fame!

On a high and open terrace with auspicious garlands graced,
Facing eastward, in his glory was the brave Sugriva placed,

Water from each holy river, from each *tirtha* famed of old,
From the broad and boundless ocean, was arranged in jars of gold,

And from vase and horn of wild bull, on their monarch and their lord,
Holy consecrating water chiefs and loyal courtiers poured.

Gaya and the great Gavaksha, Gandha-madan proud and brave,
Hanuman held up the vases, Jambaman his succour gave,

And they laved the king Sugriva as Immortals in the sky,
Consecrate the star-eyed INDRA in his mansions bright and high,

And a shout of joy and triumph, like the pealing voice of war,
Spake Sugriva's consecration to the creatures near and far!

Duteous still to Rama's mandate, as his first born and his own,
King Sugriva named young Angad sharer of his royal throne,

Gay and bannered town Kishkindha hailed Sugriva's gracious word,
Tender Tara wiped her tear-drops bowing to a younger lord!

V

The Rains in the Nilgiri Mountains

"Mark the shadowing rain and tempest," Rama to his brother said,
As on Malaya's cloud-capped ranges in their hermit-guise they strayed,

"Massive clouds like rolling mountains gather thick and gather high,
Lurid lightnings glint and sparkle, pealing thunders shake the sky,

Pregnant with the ocean moisture by the solar ray instilled,
Now the skies like fruitful mothers are with grateful waters filled!

Mark the folds of cloudy masses, ladder-like of smooth ascent,
One could almost reach the Sun-god, wreathe him with a wreath of scent,

And when glow these heavy masses red and white with evening's glow,
One could almost deem them sword-cuts branded by some heavenly foe!

Mark the streaks of golden lustre lighting up the checkered sky,
Like a lover *chandan*-painted in each breeze it heaves a sigh,

And the earth is hot and feverish, moistened with the tears of rain,
Sighing like my anguished Sita when she wept in woe and pain!

Fresh and sweet like draught of nectar is the rain-besprinkled breeze,
Fragrant with the *ketak* blossom, scented by the camphor trees,

Fresh and bold each peak and mountain bathed in soft descending rain,
So they sprinkle holy water when they bless a monarch's reign!

Fair and tall as holy hermits, stand yon shadow-mantled hills,
Murmuring *mantras* with the zephyr, robed in threads of sparkling rills,

Fair and young as gallant coursers neighing forth their thunder cries,
Lashed by golden whips of lightning are the dappled sunlit skies!

Ah, my lost and loving Sita ! writhing in a Raksha's power,
As the lightning shakes and quivers in this dark tempestuous
 shower,

Shadows thicken on the prospect, flower and leaf are wet with rain,
And each passing object, Lakshman, wakes in me a thought of
 pain !

Joyously from throne and empire with my Sita I could part,
As the stream erodes its margin, Sita's absence breaks my heart,

Rain and tempest cloud the prospect as they cloud my onward
 path,
Dubious is my darksome future, mighty is my foeman's wrath !

Ravan monarch of the Rakshas,—so Jatayu said and died,—
In some unknown forest fastness doth my sorrowing Sita hide,

But Sugriva true and faithful seeks the Raksha's secret hold,
Firm in faith and fixed in purpose we will face our foeman bold !"

VI

The Quest for Sita

Past the rains, the marshalled Vanars gathered round Sugriva bold,
And unto a gallant chieftain thus the king his purpose told :

"Brave in war and wise in counsel ! take ten thousand of my best,
Seek the hiding-place of Ravan in the regions of the East.

Seek each ravine rock and forest and each shadowy hill and cave,
Far where bright Sarayu's waters mix with Ganga's ruddy wave,

And where Jumna's dark blue waters ceaseless roll in regal pride,
And the Sone through leagues of country spreads its torrent far
 and wide.

Seek where in Videha's empire castled towns and hamlets shine,
In Kosala and in Malwa and by Kasi's sacred shrine,

Magadh rich in peopled centres, Pundra region of the brave,
Anga rich in corn and cattle on the eastern ocean wave.

Seek where clans of skilful weavers dwell upon the eastern shore,
And from virgin mines of silver miners work the sparkling ore,

In the realms of uncouth nations, in the islets of the sea,
In the mountains of the ocean, wander far and wander free !"

Next to Nila son of AGNI, Jambaman VIDHATA's son,
Hanuman the son of MARUT, famed for deeds of valour done,

Unto Gaya and Gavaksha, Gandha-madan true and tried,
Unto Angad prince and regent, thus the brave Sugriva cried :

"Noblest, bravest of our chieftains, greatest of our race are ye,
Seek and search the Southern regions, rock and ravine, wood and tree,

Search the thousand peaks of Vindhya lifting high its misty head,
Through the gorges of Narmada rolling o'er its rocky bed,

By the gloomy Godavari and by Krishna's wooded stream,
Through Utkala's sea-girt forest tinged by morning's early gleam,

Search the towns of famed Dasarna and Avanti's rocky shore,
And the uplands of Vidarbha and the mountains of Mysore,

Land of Matsyas and Kalingas and Kausika's regions fair,
Trackless wilderness of Dandak seek with anxious toil and care.

Search the empire of the Andhras, of the sister-nations three,—
Cholas, Cheras and the Pandyas dwelling by the southern sea,

Pass Kaveri's spreading waters, Malya's mountains towering brave,
Seek the isle of Tamra-parni, gemmed upon the ocean wave !"

To Susena chief and elder,—Tara's noble sire was he,—
Spake Sugriva with obeisance and the accents bold and free :

"Take my lord, a countless army of the bravest and the best,
Search where beats the sleepless ocean on the regions of the West.

Search the country of Saurashtras, of Bahlikas strong and brave,
And each busy mart and seaport on the western ocean wave,

Castles girt by barren mountains, deserts by the sandy sea,
Forests of the fragrant *ketak*, regions of the *tamal* tree!

Search the ocean port of Pattan shaded by its fruitful trees,
Where the feathery groves of cocoa court the balmy western
breeze,

Where on peaks of Soma-giri lordly lions wander free,
Where the waters of the Indus mingle with the mighty sea!"

Lastly to the valiant chieftain Satavala strong and brave,
For the quest of saintly Sita thus his mighty mandate gave:

"Hie thee, gallant Satavala, with thy forces wander forth,
To the peaks of Himalaya, to the regions of the North!

Mlechchas and the wild Pulindas in the rocky regions dwell,
Madra chiefs and mighty Kurus live within each fertile vale,

Wild Kambojas of the mountains, Yavanas of wondrous skill,
Sakas swooping from their gorges, Pattanas of iron will!

Search the woods of *devadaru* mantling Himalaya's side,
And the forests of the *lodhra* spreading in their darksome pride,

Search the land of Soma-srma where the gay *Gandharvas* dwell,
In the table land of Kala search each rock and ravine well!

Cross the snowy Himalaya, and Sudarsan's holy peak,
Deva-sakha's wooded ranges which the feathered songsters seek,

Cross the vast and dreary region void of stream or wooded hill,
Till you reach the white Kailasa, home of Gods, serene and still!

Pass Kuvera's pleasant regions, search the Krauncha mountain well,
And the land where warlike females and the horse-faced women
dwell,

Halt not till you reach the country where the Northern Kurus rest,
Utmost confines of the wide earth, home of Gods and Spirits
blest!"

BOOK VIII

SITA-SANDESA

(*Sita Discovered*)

Among the many chiefs sent by Sugriva in different directions in search of Sita, Hanuman succeeded in the quest and discovered Sita in Ceylon. Ceylon is separated from India by a broad channel of the sea, and Hanuman leaped, or rather flew through the air, across the channel and lighted on the island. Sita, scorning the proposals of Ravan, was kept in confinement in a garden of *Asoka* trees, surrounded by a terrible guard of Raksha females; and in this hard confinement she remained true and faithful to her lord. Hanuman gave her a token from Rama, and carried back to Rama a token which she sent of her undying affection and truth.

The portions translated in this Book form the whole of the main portions of Sections xv., xxxi., xxxvi., and lxvi. of Book v. of the original text.

I

Sita in the Asoka Garden

Crossed the ocean's boundless waters, Hanuman in duty brave,
Lighted on the emerald island girdled by the sapphire wave,

And in tireless quest of Sita searched the margin of the sea,
In a dark *Asoka* garden hid himself within a tree.

Creepers threw their clasping tendrils round the trees of ample height,
Stately palm and feathered cocoa, fruit and blossom pleased the sight,

Herds of tame and gentle creatures in the grassy meadow strayed,
Kokils sang in leafy thicket, birds of plumage lit the shade,

Limpid lakes of scented lotus with their fragrance filled the air,
Homes and huts of rustic beauty peeped through bushes green and fair,

Blossoms rich in tint and fragrance in the checkered shadow gleamed,
Clustering fruits of golden beauty in the yellow sunlight beamed!

Brightly shone the red *Asoka* with the morning's golden ray,
Karnikara and *Kinsuka* dazzling as the light of day,

Brightly grew the flower of *Champak* in the vale and on the reef,
Punnaga and *Saptaparna* with its seven-fold scented leaf,

Rich in blossoms many tinted, grateful to the ravished eye,
Gay and green and glorious Lanka was like garden of the sky,

Rich in fruit and laden creeper and in beauteous bush and tree,
Flower-bespangled golden Lanka was like gem-bespangled sea!

Rose a palace in the woodlands girt by pillars strong and high,
Snowy-white like fair Kailasa cleaving through the azure sky,

And its steps were ocean coral and its pavement yellow gold,
White and gay and heaven-aspiring rose the structure high and bold!

By the rich and royal mansion Hanuman his eyes did rest,
On a woman sad and sorrowing in her sylvan garments drest,

Like the moon obscured and clouded, dim with shadows deep and dark,
Like the smoke-enshrouded red fire, dying with a feeble spark,

Like the tempest-pelted lotus by the wind and torrent shaken,
Like the beauteous star Rohini by a *graha* overtaken!

Fasts and vigils paled her beauty, tears bedimmed her tender grace,
Anguish dwelt within her bosom, sorrow darkened on her face,

And she lived by Rakshas guarded, as a faint and timid deer,
Severed from her herd and kindred when the prowling wolves are near,

And her raven locks ungathered hung behind in single braid,
And her gentle eye was lightless, and her brow was hid in shade!

"This is she! the peerless princess, Rama's consort loved and lost,
This is she! the saintly Sita, by a cruel fortune crost,"

Hanuman thus thought and pondered: "On her graceful form I spy,
Gems and gold by sorrowing Rama oft depicted with a sigh,

On her ears the golden pendants and the tiger's sharpened tooth,
On her arms the jewelled bracelets, tokens of unchanging truth,

On her pallid brow and bosom still the radiant jewels shine,
Rama with a sweet affection did in early days entwine!

Hermit's garments clothe her person, braided is her raven hair,
Matted bark of trees of forest drape her neck and bosom fair,

And a dower of dazzling beauty still bedecks her peerless face,
Though the shadowing tinge of sorrow darkens all her earlier grace!

This is she! the soft-eyed Sita, wept with unavailing tear,
This is she! the faithful consort, unto Rama ever dear,

Unforgetting and unchanging, truthful still in deed and word,
Sita in her silent suffering sorrows for her absent lord,

Still for Rama lost but cherished, Sita heaves the choking sigh,
Sita lives for righteous Rama, for her Rama she would die!"

II

The Voice of Hope

Hanuman from leafy shelter lifts his voice in sacred song,
Till the tale of Rama's glory Lanka's woods and vales prolong:

"Listen, Lady, to my story ;—Dasa-ratha famed in war,
Rich in steeds and royal tuskers, armèd men and battle car,

Ruled his realm in truth and virtue, in his bounty ever free,
Of the mighty race of Raghu mightiest king and monarch he,

Robed in every royal virtue, great in peace in battle brave,
Blest in bliss of grateful nations, blest in blessings which he gave!

And his eldest-born and dearest, Rama soul of righteous might,
Shone, as mid the stars resplendent shines the radiant Lord of
Night,

True unto his sacred duty, true unto his kith and kin,
Friend of piety and virtue, punisher of crime and sin,

Loved in all his spacious empire, peopled mart and hermit's den,
With a truer deeper kindness Rama loved his subject men!

Dasa-ratha, promise-fettered, then his cruel mandate gave,
Rama with his wife and brother lived in woods and rocky cave,

And he slayed the deer of jungle and he slept in leafy shade,
Stern destroyer of the Rakshas in the pathless forests strayed,

Till the monarch of the Rakshas,—fraudful is his impious life,—
Cheated Rama in the jungle, from his cottage stole his wife!

Long lamenting lone and weary Rama wandered in the wood,
Searched for Sita in the jungle where his humble cottage stood,

Godavari's gloomy gorges, Krishna's dark and wooded shore,
And the ravine, rock and valley, and the cloud-capped mountain
hoar!

Then he met the sad Sugriva in wild Malya's dark retreat,
Won for him his father's empire and his father's royal seat,

Now Sugriva's countless forces wander far and wander near,
In the search of stolen Sita still unto his Rama dear!

I am henchman of Sugriva and the mighty sea have crost,
In the quest of hidden Sita, Rama's consort loved and lost,

And methinks that form of beauty, peerless shape of woman's grace,
Is my Rama's dear-loved consort, Rama's dear-remembered face!"

Hushed the voice; the ravished Sita cast her wond'ring eyes around,
Whence that song of sudden gladness, whence that soul-entrancing sound?

Dawning hope and rising rapture overflowed her widowed heart,
Is it dream's deceitful whisper which the cruel Fates impart?

III

Rama's Token

" 'Tis no dream's deceitful whisper!" Hanuman spake to the dame,
As from darksome leafy shelter he to Rama's consort came,

"Rama's messenger and vassal, token from thy lord I bring,
Mark this bright ring, jewel-lettered with the dear name of thy king,

For the loved and cherished Sita is to Rama ever dear,
And he sends his loving message and his force is drawing near!"

Sita held that tender token from her loved and cherished lord,
And once more herself she fancied to his loving arms restored,

And her pallid face was lighted and her soft eye sent a spark,
As the Moon regains her lustre freed from *Rahu's* shadows dark!

And with voice of deep emotion in each softly whispered word,
Spake her thoughts in gentle accents of her consort and her lord:

"Messenger of love of Rama! Dauntless is thy deed and bold,
Thou hast crossed the boundless ocean to the Raksha's castled hold.

Thou hast crossed the angry billows which confess no monarch's sway,
O'er the face of rolling waters found thy unresisted way,

Thou hast done what living mortal never sought to do before,
Dared the Raksha in his island, Ravan in his sea-girt shore!

Speak, if Rama lives in safety in the woods or by the hill,
And if young and gallant Lakshman faithful serves his brother
still,

Speak, if Rama in his anger and his unforgiving ire,
Hurls destruction on my captor like the world-consuming fire,

Speak, if Rama in his sorrow wets his pale and drooping eye,
If the thought of absent Sita wakes within his heart a sigh!

Doth my husband seek alliance with each wild and warlike chief,
Striving for a speedy vengeance and for Sita's quick relief,

Doth he stir the warlike races to a fierce and vengeful strife,
Dealing death to ruthless Rakshas for this insult on his wife,

Doth he still in fond remembrance cherish Sita loved of yore,
Nursing in his hero-bosom tender sorrows evermore?

Didst thou hear from far Ayodhya, from Kausalya royal dame,
From the true and tender Bharat prince of proud and peerless fame,

Didst thou hear if royal Bharat leads his forces to the fight,
Conquering Ravan's scattered army in his all-resistless might,

Didst thou hear if brave Sugriva marshals Vanars in his wrath,
And the young and gallant Lakshman seeks to cross the ocean
path?"

Hanuman with due obeisance placed his hand upon his head,
Bowed unto the queenly Sita and in gentle accents said:

"Trust me, Lady, valiant Rama soon will greet his saintly wife,
E'en as INDRA greets his goddess, SACHI dearer than his life,

Trust me, Sita, conquering Rama comes with panoply of war,
Shaking Lanka's sea-girt mountains, slaying Rakshas near and far!

He shall cross the boundless ocean with the battle's dread array,
He shall smite the impious Ravan and the cruel Rakshas slay,

Mighty Gods and strong Asuras shall not hinder Rama's path,
When at Lanka's gates he thunders with his more than godlike
wrath,

Deadly YAMA, all-destroying, pales before his peerless might,
When his red right arm of vengeance wrathful Rama lifts to smite!

By the lofty Mandar mountains, by the fruit and root I seek,
By the cloud-obstructing Vindhyas, and by Malya's towering peak,

I will swear, my gentle Lady, Rama's vengeance draweth nigh,
Thou shalt see his beaming visage like the Lord of Midnight Sky,

Firm in purpose Rama waiteth on the Prasra-vana hill,
As upon the huge Airavat, INDRA, motionless and still!

Flesh of deer nor forest honey tasteth Rama true and bold,
Till he rescues cherished Sita from the Raksha's castled hold,

Thoughts of Sita leave not Rama dreary day or darksome night,
Till his vengeance deep and dreadful crushes Ravan in his might,

Forest flower nor scented creeper pleases Rama's anguished heart,
Till he wins his wedded consort by his death-compelling dart!"

IV

SITA'S TOKEN

Token from her raven tresses Sita to the Vanar gave,
Hanuman with dauntless valour crossed once more the ocean wave,

Where in Prasra-vana's mountain Rama with his brother stayed,
Jewel from the brow of Sita by her sorrowing consort laid,

Spake of Ravan's foul endearment and his loathsome loving word,
Spake of Sita's scorn and anger and her truth unto her lord,

Tears of sorrow and affection from the warrior's eyelids start,
As his consort's loving token Rama presses to his heart!

"As the mother-cow, Sugriva, yields her milk beside her young,
Welling tears upon this token yields my heart by anguish wrung,

Well I know this dear-loved jewel sparkling with the ray of heaven,
Born in sea, by mighty INDRA to my Sita's father given,

Well I know this tender token, Janak placed it on her hair,
When she came my bride and consort decked in beauty rich and rare,

Well I know this sweet memorial, Sita wore it on her head,
And her proud and peerless beauty on the gem a lustre shed!

Ah, methinks the gracious Janak stands again before my eye,
With a father's fond affection, with a monarch's stature high,

Ah, methinks my bride and consort, she who wore it on her brow,
Stands again before the altar speaks again her loving vow,

Ah, the sad the sweet remembrance! Ah, the happy days gone by,
Once again, O loving vision, wilt thou gladden Rama's eye?

Speak again, my faithful vassal, how my Sita wept and prayed,
Like the water to the thirsty, dear to me what Sita said,

Did she send this sweet remembrance as a blessing from above,
As a true and tender token of a woman's changeless love,

Did she waft her heart's affection o'er the billows of the sea,
Wherefore came she not in person from her foes and fetters free?

Hanuman, my friend and comrade, lead me to the distant isle,
Where my soft-eyed Sita lingers midst the Rakshas dark and vile,

Where my true and tender consort like a lone and stricken deer,
Girt by Rakshas stern and ruthless sheds the unavailing tear,

Where she weeps in ceaseless anguish, sorrow-stricken sad and pale,
Like the Moon by dark clouds shrouded then her light and lustre fail!

Speak again, my faithful henchman, loving message of my wife,
Like some potent drug her accents renovate my fainting life,

Arm thy forces, friend Sugriva, Rama shall not brook delay,
While in distant Lanka's confines Sita weeps the livelong day,

Marshal forth thy bannered forces, cross the ocean in thy might,
Rama speeds on wings of vengeance Lanka's impious lord to smite!"

BOOK IX

RAVANA SABHA

(*The Council of War*)

Ravan was thoroughly frightened by the deeds of Hanuman. For Hanuman had not only penetrated into his island and discovered Sita in her imprisonment, but had also managed to burn down a great portion of the city before he left the island. Ravan called a Council of War, and as might be expected, all the advisers heedlessly advised war.

All but Bibhishan. He was the youngest brother of Ravan, and condemned the folly and the crime by which Ravan was seeking a war with the righteous and unoffending Rama. He advised that Sita should be restored to her lord and peace made with Rama. His voice was drowned in the cries of more violent advisers.

It is noticeable that Ravan's second brother, Kumbha-karna, also had the courage to censure his elder's action. But unlike Bibhishan he was determined to fight for his king whether he was right or wrong. There is a touch of sublimity in this blind and devoted loyalty of Kumbha-karna to the cause of his king and his country.

Bibhishan was driven from the court with indignity, and joined the forces of Rama, to whom he gave much valuable information about Lanka and its warriors.

The passages translated in this Book form Sections vi., viii., ix., portions of Sections xii., and xv., and the whole of Section xvi., of Book vi. of the original text.

I

RAVAN SEEKS ADVICE

Monarch of the mighty Rakshas, Ravan spake to warriors all,
Spake to gallant chiefs and princes gathered in his Council Hall:

"Listen, Princes, Chiefs and Warriors! Hanuman our land hath seen,
Stealing through the woods of Lanka unto Rama's prisoned queen,

And audacious in his purpose and resistless in his ire,
Burnt our turret tower and temple, wasted Lanka's town with fire!

Speak your counsel, gallant leaders, Ravan is intent to hear,
Triumph waits on fearless wisdom, speak your thoughts without a fear,

Wisest monarchs act on counsel from his men for wisdom known,
Next are they who in their wisdom and their daring act alone,

Last, unwisest are the monarchs who nor death nor danger weigh,
Think not, ask not friendly counsel, by their passions borne away!

Wisest counsel comes from courtiers who in holy lore unite,
Next, when varying plans and reasons blending lead unto the right,

Last and worst, when stormy passions mark the hapless king's debate,
And his friends are disunited when his foe is at the gate!

Therefore freely speak your counsel and your monarch's task shall be,
But to shape in deed and action what your wisest thoughts decree,

Speak with minds and hearts united, shape your willing monarch's deed,
Counsel peace, or Ravan's forces to a war of vengeance lead,

Ere Sugriva's countless forces cross the vast and boundless main,
Ere the wrathful Rama girdles Lanka with a living chain!"

II

Prahasta's Speech

Dark and high as summer tempest mighty-armed Prahasta rose,
Spake in fierce and fiery accents hurling challenge on his foes:

"Wherefore, Ravan, quails thy bosom, gods against thee strive in vain,
Wherefore fear the feeble mortals, homeless hermits, helpless men?

Hanuman approached in secret, stealing like a craven spy,
Not from me in open combat would alive the Vanar fly,

Let him come with all his forces, to the confines of the sea,
I will chase the scattered army and thy town from foemen free!

Not in fear and hesitation Ravan should repent his deed,
While his gallant Raksha forces stand beside him in his need,

Not in tears and vain repentance Sita to his consort yield,
While his chieftains guard his empire in the battle's gory field!"

III

Durmukha's Speech

Durmukha of cruel visage and of fierce and angry word,
Rose within the Council Chamber, spake to Lanka's mighty lord:

"Never shall the wily foeman boast of insult on us flung,
Hanuman shall die a victim for the outrage and the wrong!

Stealing in unguarded Lanka through thy city's virgin gate,
He hath courted deep disaster and a dark untimely fate,

Stealing in the inner mansions where our dames and damsels dwell,
Hanuman shall die a victim,—tale of shame he shall not tell!

Need is none of Ravan's army, bid me seek the foe alone,
If he hides in sky or ocean or in nether regions thrown,

Need is none of gathered forces, Ravan's mandate I obey,
I will smite the bold intruder and his Vanar forces slay!"

IV

Vajra-danshtra's Speech

Iron toothed Vajra-danshtra then arose in wrath and pride,
And his blood-stained mace of battle held in fury by his side:

"Wherefore, Ravan, waste thy forces on the foemen poor and vile,
Hermit Rama and his brother, Hanuman of impious wile,

Bid me,—with this mace of battle proud Sugriva I will slay,
Chase the helpless hermit brothers to the forests far away!

Or to deeper counsel listen! Varied shapes the Rakshas wear,
Let them, wearing human visage, dressed as Bharat's troops appear,

Succour from his ruling brother Rama will in gladness greet,
Then with mace and blood-stained sabre we shall lay them at our feet,

Rock and javelin and arrow we shall on our foemen hail,
Till no poor surviving Vanar lives to tell the tragic tale!"

V

Speech of Nikumbha and Vajra-hanu

Then arose the brave Nikumbha,—Kumbha-karna's son was he,—
Spake his young heart's mighty passion in his accents bold and free:

"Need is none, O mighty monarch, for a battle or a war,
Bid me meet the homeless Rama and his brother wand'ring far,

Bid me face the proud Sugriva, Hanuman of deepest wile,
I will rid thee of thy foemen and of Vanars poor and vile!"

Rose the chief with jaw of iron, Vajra-hanu fierce and young,
Licked his lips like hungry tiger with his red and lolling tongue:

"Wherefore, monarch, dream of battle? Rakshas feed on human gore,
Let me feast upon thy foemen by the ocean's lonely shore,

Rama and his hermit brother, Hanuman who hides in wood,
Angad and the proud Sugriva soon shall be my welcome food!"

VI

Bibhishan's Warning

Twenty warriors armed and girded in the Council Hall arose,
Thirsting for a war of vengeance, hurling challenge on the foes,

But Bibhishan deep in wisdom,—Ravan's youngest brother he,—
Spake the word of solemn warning for his eye could farthest see:

"Pardon, king and honoured elder, if Bibhishan lifts his voice,
'Gainst the wishes of the warriors and the monarch's fatal choice,

Firm in faith and strong in forces Rama comes with conqu'ring might,
Vain against a righteous warrior would unrighteous Ravan fight!

Think him not a common Vanar who transpassed the ocean wave,
Wrecked thy city tower and temple and a sign and warning gave,

Think him not a common hermit who Ayodhya ruled of yore,
Crossing India's streams and mountains, thunders now on Lanka's shore!

What dark deed of crime or folly hath the righteous Rama done,
That you stole his faithful consort unprotected and alone,

What offence or nameless insult hath the saintly Sita given,
She who chained in Lanka's prison pleads in piteous tears to Heaven?

Take my counsel, king and elder, Sita to her lord restore,
Wipe this deed of wrong and outrage, Rama's righteous grace implore,

Take my counsel, Raksha monarch, vain against him is thy might,
Doubly armèd is the hero,—he who battles for the right!

Render Sita to her Rama ere with vengeance swift and dire,
He despoils our peopled Lanka with his bow and brand and fire,

Render wife unto her husband ere in battle's dread array,
Rama swoops upon thy empire like a falcon on its prey,

Render to the lord his consort ere with blood of Rakshas slain,
Rama soaks the land of Lanka to the margin of the main!

Listen to my friendly counsel,—though it be I stand alone,—
Faithful friend but fiery foeman is this Dasa-ratha's son,

Listen to my voice of warning,—Rama's shafts are true and keen,
Flaming like the with'ring sunbeams on the summer's parchèd green,

Listen to my soft entreaty,—righteousness becomes the brave,
Cherish peace and cherish virtue and thy sons and daughters
save!"

VII

Kumbha-karna's Determination

Ravan's brother Kumbha-karna, from his wonted slumber woke,
Mightiest he of all the Rakshas, thus in solemn accents spoke:

"Truly speaks the wise Bibhishan; ere he stole a hermit's wife,
Ravan should have thought and pondered, courted not a causeless strife,

Ere he did this deed of folly, Ravan should have counsel sought,
Tardy is the vain repentance when the work of shame is wrought!

Word of wisdom timely spoken saves from death and dangers dire,
Vain is grief for crime committed,—offerings to unholy fire,

Vain is hero's worth or valour if by foolish counsel led,
Toil and labour fail and perish save when unto wisdom wed,

And the foeman speeds in triumph o'er a heedless monarch's might,
As through gaps of Krauncha mountains *hansas* speed their
southern flight!

Ravan, thou hast sought unwisely Sita in her calm retreat,
As the wild and heedless hunter feeds upon the poisoned meat,

Nathless, faithful Kumbha-karna will his loyal duty know,
He shall fight his monarch's battle, he shall face his brother's foe!

True to brother and to monarch, be he right or be he wrong,
Kumbha-karna fights for Lanka 'gainst her foemen fierce and
strong,

Recks not if the mighty Indra and Vivasvat cross his path,
Or the wild and stormy Maruts, Agni in his fiery wrath!

For the Lord of Sky shall tremble when he sees my stature high,
And he hears his thunders echoed by my loud and answering cry,

Rama armed with ample quiver shall no second arrow send,
Ere I slay him in the battle and his limb from limb I rend!

Wiser heads than Kumbha-karna right and true from wrong may know,
Faithful to his race and monarch he shall face the haughty foe,

Joy thee in thy pleasures, Ravan, rule thy realm in regal pride,
When I slay the hermit Rama, widowed Sita be thy bride!"

VIII

Indrajit's Assurance

Indrajit the son of Ravan then his lofty purpose told,
Midst the best and boldest Rakshas none so gallant, none so bold,

"Wherefore, noble king and father, pale Bibhishan's counsel hear,
Scion of the race of Rakshas speaks not thus in dastard fear,

In this race of valiant Rakshas, known for deeds of glory done,
Feeble-hearted, faint in courage, save Bibhishan, there is none!

Matched with meanest of the Rakshas what are sons of mortal men,
What are homeless human brothers hiding in the hermit's den,

Shall we yield to weary wand'rers, driven from their distant home,
Chased from throne and father's kingdom in the desert woods to roam?

Lord of sky and nether regions, Indra 'neath my weapon fell,
Pale Immortals know my valour and my warlike deeds can tell,

Indra's tusker, huge Airávat, by my prowess overthrown,
Trumpeted its anguished accents, shaking sky and earth with groan,

Mighty Gods and dauntless Daityas fame of Indrajit may know,
And he yields not, king and father, to a homeless human foe!"

IX

Ravan's Decision

Anger swelled in Ravan's bosom as he cast his blood-red eye,
On Bibhishan calm and fearless, and he spake in accents high:

"Rather dwell with open foemen or in homes where cobras haunt,
Than with faithless friends who falter and whom fears of danger daunt!

O, the love of near relations!—false and faithless, full of guile,—
How they sorrow at my glory, at my danger how they smile,

How they grieve with secret anguish when my loftier virtues shine,
How they harbour jealous envy when deserts and fame are mine,

How they scan with curious vision every fault that clouds my path,
How they wait with eager longing till I fall in Fortune's wrath!

Ask the elephants of jungle how their captors catch and bind,—
Not by fire and feeble weapons, but by treason of their kind,

Not by javelin or arrow,—little for these arms they care,—
But their false and fondling females lead them to the hunter's snare!

Long as nourishment and vigour shall impart the milk of cow,
Long as women shall be changeful, hermits holy in their vow,

Aye, so long shall near relations hate us in their inner mind,
Mark us with a secret envy though their words be ne'er so kind!

Rain-drops fall upon the lotus but unmingling hang apart,
False relations round us gather but they blend not heart with heart,

Winter clouds are big with thunder but they shed no freshening rain,
False relations smile and greet us but their soothing words are vain,

Bees are tempted by the honey but from flower to flower they range,
False relations share our favour but in secret seek a change!

Lying is thy speech, Bibhishan, secret envy lurks within,
Thou wouldst rule thy elder's empire, thou wouldst wed thy elder's queen,

Take thy treason to the foemen,—brother's blood I may not shed,—
Other Raksha craven-hearted by my royal hands had bled!"

X

Bibhishan's Departure

"This to me!" Bibhishan answered, as with fiery comrades four,
Rose in arms the wrathful Raksha and in fury rushed before,

"But I spare thee, royal Ravan angry words thy lips have passed,
False and lying and unfounded is the censure thou hast cast!

True Bibhishan sought thy safety, strove to save his elder's reign,—
Speed thee now to thy destruction since all counsel is in vain,

Many are thy smiling courtiers who with honeyed speech beguile,—
Few are they with truth and candour speak their purpose void of guile!

Blind to reason and to wisdom, Ravan, seek thy destined fate,
For thy impious lust of woman, for thy dark unrighteous hate,

Blind to danger and destruction, deaf to word of counsel given,
By the flaming shafts of Rama thou shalt die by will of Heaven!

Yet, O! yet, my king and elder, let me plead with latest breath,
'Gainst the death of race and kinsmen, 'gainst my lord and brother's death,

Ponder yet, O Raksha monarch, save thy race and save thy own,
Ravan, part we now for ever,—guard thy ancient sea-girt throne!"

BOOK X

YUDDHA

(*The War in Ceylon*)

Rama crossed over with his army from India to Ceylon. There is a chain of islands across the strait, and the Indian poet supposes them to be the remains of a vast causeway which Rama built to cross over with his army.

The town of Lanka, the capital of Ceylon, was invested, and the war which followed was a succession of sallies by the great leaders and princes of Lanka. But almost every sally was repulsed, every chief was killed, and at last Ravan himself who made the last sally was slain and the war ended.

Among the numberless fights described in the original work, those of Ravan himself, his brother Kumbha-karna, and his son Indrajit, are the most important, and often recited and listened to in India; and these have been rendered into English in this Book. And the reader will mark a certain method in the poet's estimate of the warriors who took part in these battles.

First and greatest among the warriors was Rama; he was never beaten by an open foe, never conquered in fair fight. Next to him, and to him only, was Ravan the monarch of Lanka; he twice defeated Lakshman in battle, and never retreated except before Rama. Next to Rama and to Ravan stood their brothers, Lakshman and Kumbha-karna; it is difficult to say who was the best of these two, for they fought only once, and it was a drawn battle. Fifth in order of prowess was Indrajit, the son of Ravan, but he was the first in his magic art. Concealed in mists by his magic, he twice defeated both Rama and Lakshman; but in his last battle he had to wage a face to face combat with Lakshman, and was slain. After these five warriors, pre-eminent for their prowess, various Vanars and Rakshas took their rank.

The war ended with the fall of Ravan and his funerals. The portions translated in this Book form the whole or portions of Sections xliv., xlviii., lix., lxvi, lxvii., and lxxiii., an abstract of Sections lxxv., to xci., and portions of Sections xciii., xcvi., ci., cii., ciii., cix., cx., and cxiii., of Book vi. of the original text.

I

Indrajit's First Battle—The Serpent-Noose

Darkly round the leaguered city Rama's countless forces lay,
Far as Ravan cast his glances in the dawning light of day,

Wrath and anguish shook his bosom and the gates he opened wide,
And with ranks of charging Rakshas sallied with a Raksha's pride!

All the day the battle lasted, endless were the tale to tell,
What unnumbered Vanars perished and what countless Rakshas fell,

Darkness came, the fiery foemen urged the still unceasing fight,
Struggling with a deathless hatred fiercer in the gloom of night!

Onward came resistless Rakshas, laid Sugriva's forces low,
Crushed the broken ranks of Vanars, drank the red blood of the foe,

Bravely fought the scattered Vanars facing still the tide of war,
Struggling with the charging tusker and the steed and battle car,

Till at last the gallant Lakshman and the godlike Rama came,
And they swept the hosts of Ravan like a sweeping forest flame,

And their shafts like hissing serpents on the falt'ring foemen fell,
Fiercer grew the sable midnight with the dying shriek and yell!

Dust arose like clouds of summer from each thunder-sounding car,
From the hoofs of charging coursers, from the elephants of war,

Streams of red blood warm and bubbling issued from the countless slain,
Flooded battle's dark arena like the floods of summer rain,

Sound of trumpet and of bugle, drum and horn and echoing shell,
And the neigh of charging coursers and the tuskers' dying wail,

And the yell of wounded Rakshas and the Vanars' fierce delight,
Shook the earth and sounding welkin, waked the echoes of the
night!

Six bright arrows Rama thundered from his weapon dark and
dread,
Iron-toothed Bajra-dranshtra and his fainting comrades fled,

Dauntless still the serried Rakshas, wave on wave succeeding came,
Perished under Rama's arrows as the moths upon the flame!

Indrajit the son of Ravan, Lanka's glory and her pride,
Matchless in his magic weapons came and turned battle's tide,

What though Angad in his fury had his steeds and driver slayed,
Indrajit hid in the midnight battled from its friendly shade,

Shrouded in a cloud of darkness still he poured his darts like rain,
On young Lakshman and on Rama and on countless Vanars slain,

Matchless in his magic weapons, then he hurled his *Naga*-dart,
Serpent noose upon his foemen draining life blood from their
heart!

Vainly then the royal brothers fought the cloud-enshrouded foe,
Vainly sought the unseen warrior dealing unresisted blow,

Fastened by a noose of *Naga* forced by hidden foe to yield,
Rama and the powerless Lakshman fell and fainted on the field!

II

Sita's Lament

Indrajit ere dawned the morning entered in his father's hall,
Spake of midnight's darksome contest, Rama's death and Laksh-
man's fall,

And the proud and peerless Ravan clasped his brave and gallant son,
Praised him for his skill and valour and his deed of glory done,

And with dark and cruel purpose bade his henchmen yoke his car,
Bade them take the sorrowing Sita to the gory field of war.

Soon they harnessed royal coursers and they took the weeping wife,
Where her Rama, pierced and bleeding, seemed bereft of sense and
life,

Brother lay beside his brother with their shattered mail and bow,
Arrows thick and dark with red blood spake the conquest of the
foe,

Anguish woke in Sita's bosom and a dimness filled her eye,
And a widow's nameless sorrow burst in widow's mournful cry:

"Rama, lord and king and husband! didst thou cross the billowy
sea,
Didst thou challenge death and danger, court thy fate to rescue me,

Didst thou hurl a fitting vengeance on the cruel Raksha force,
Till the hand of hidden foeman checked thy all-resistless course?

Breathes upon the earth no warrior who could face thee in the
fight,
Who could live to boast his triumph o'er thy world-subduing might,

But the will of Fate is changeless, Death is mighty in his sway,—
Peerless Rama, faithful Lakshman, sleep the sleep that knows no
day!

But I weep not for my Rama nor for Lakshman young and brave,
They have done a warrior's duty and have found a warrior's grave,

And I weep not for my sorrows,—sorrow marked me from my
birth,—
Child of Earth I seek in suffering bosom of my mother Earth!

But I grieve for dear Kausalya, sonless mother, widowed queen,
How she reckons days and seasons in her anguish ever green,

How she waits with eager longing till her Rama's exile o'er,
He would soothe her lifelong sorrow, bless her aged eyes once
more,

Sita's love! Ayodhya's monarch! queen Kausalya's dearest born!
Rama soul of truth and virtue sleeps the sleep that knows no
morn!"

Sorely wept the sorrowing Sita in her accents soft and low,
And the silent stars of midnight wept to witness Sita's woe,

But Trijata her companion,—though a Raksha woman she,—
Felt her soul subdued by sadness, spake to Sita tenderly:

"Weep not, sad and saintly Sita, shed not widow's tears in vain,
For thy lord is sorely wounded, but shall live to fight again,

Rama and the gallant Lakshman, fainting, not bereft of life,
They shall live to fight and conquer,—thou shalt be a happy wife.

Mark the Vanars' marshalled forces, listen to their warlike cries,
'Tis not thus the soldiers gather when a chief and hero dies,

'Tis not thus round lifeless leader muster warriors true and brave,
For when falls the dying helmsman, sinks the vessel in the wave!

Mark the ring of hopeful Vanars, how they watch o'er Rama's face,
How they guard the younger Lakshman beaming yet with living grace,

Trust me, sad and sorrowing Sita, marks of death these eyes can trace,
Shade of death's decaying fingers sweeps not o'er thy Rama's face!

Listen more, my gentle Sita, though a captive in our keep,
For thy woes and for thy anguish see a Raksha woman weep,

Though thy Rama armed in battle is our unrelenting foe,
For a true and stainless warrior see a Raksha filled with woe!

Fainting on the field of battle, blood-ensanguined in their face,
They shall live to fight and conquer, worthy of their gallant race,

Cold not rigid are their features, darkness dwells not on their brow,
Weep not thus, my gentle Sita,—hasten we to Lanka now."

And Trijata spake no falsehood, by the winged Garuda's skill,
Rama and the valiant Lakshman lived to fight their foemen still!

III

Ravan's First Battle—The Javelin-Stroke

'Gainst the God-assisted Rama, Ravan's efforts all were vain,
Leaguered Lanka vainly struggled in her adamantine chain,

Wrathful Rakshas with their forces vainly issued through the gate,
Chiefs and serried ranks of warriors met the same resistless fate!

Dark-eyed chief Dhumraksha sallied with the fierce tornado's
shock,
Hanuman of peerless prowess slayed him with a rolling rock,

Iron-toothèd Vajra-danshtra dashed through countless Vanars slain,
But the young and gallant Angad laid him lifeless on the plain,

Akampan unshaken warrior issued out of Lanka's wall,
Hanuman was true and watchful, speedy was the Raksha's fall,

Then the mighty-armed Prahasta strove to break the hostile line,
But the gallant Nila felled him as the woodman fells the pine!

Bravest chiefs and countless soldiers sallied forth to face the fight,
Broke not Rama's iron circle, 'scaped not Rama's wond'rous might,

Ravan could no longer tarry for his mightiest chiefs were slain,
Foremost leaders, dearest kinsmen, lying on the gory plain!

"Lofty scorn of foes unworthy spared them from my flaming ire,
But the blood of slaughtered kinsmen claims from me a vengeance
dire,"

Speaking thus the wrathful Ravan mounted on his thundering car,
Flame-resplendent was the chariot drawn by matchless steeds of
war!

Beat of drum and voice of *sankha* and the Raksha's battle cry,
Song of triumph, chanted *mantra*, smote the echoing vault of sky,

And the troops like cloudy masses with their eyes of lightning fire,
Girt their monarch, as his legions girdle Rudra in his ire!

Rolled the car with peal of thunder through the city's lofty gate,
And each fierce and fiery Raksha charged with warrior's deathless
hate,

And the vigour of the onset cleft the stunned and scattered foe,
As a strong bark cleaves the billows riding on the ocean's brow !

Brave Sugriva king of Vanars met the foeman fierce and strong,
And a rock with mighty effort on the startled Ravan flung,

Vain the toil, disdainful Ravan dashed aside the flying rock,
Brave Sugriva pierced by arrows fainted neath the furious shock,

Next Susena chief and elder, Nala and Gavaksha bold,
Hurled them on the path of Ravan speeding in his car of gold,

Vainly heaved the rock and missile, vainly did with trees assail,
Onward sped the conquering Ravan, pierced the fainting Vanars
fell.

Hanuman the son of MARUT next against the Raksha came,
Fierce and strong as stormy MARUT, warrior of unrivalled fame,

But the Raksha's mighty onset gods nor mortals might sustain,
Hanuman in red blood welt'ring rolled upon the gory plain.

Onward rolled the car of Ravan, where the dauntless Nila stood,
Armed with rock and tree and missile, thirsting for the Raksha's
blood,

Vainly fought the valiant Nila, pierced by Ravan's pointed dart,
On the gory field of battle pored the red blood of his heart.

Onward through the scattered forces Ravan's conquering chariot
came,
Where in pride and dauntless valour Lakshman stood of warlike
fame,

Calm and proud the gallant Lakshman marked the all-resistless foe,
Boldly challenged Lanka's monarch as he held aloft his bow :

"Welcome, mighty Lord of Lanka ! wage with me an equal strife,
Wherefore with thy royal prowess seek the humble Vanars' life ?"

"Hath thy fate," so answered Ravan, "brought thee to thy deadly
foe,
Welcome, valiant son of Raghu! Ravan longs to lay thee low!"

Then they closed in dubious battle, Lanka's Lord his weapon bent,
Seven bright arrows, keen and whistling, on the gallant Lakshman
sent,

Vain the toil, for watchful Lakshman stout of heart and true of
aim,
With his darts like shooting sunbeams cleft each arrow as it came.

Bleeding from the darts of Lakshman, pale with anger, wounded
sore,
Ravan drew at last his *Sakti*, gift of Gods in days of yore,

Javelin of flaming splendour, deadly like the shaft of Fate,
Ravan hurled on dauntless Lakshman in his fierce and furious hate.

Vain were Lakshman's human weapons aimed with skill directed
well,
Pierced by *Sakti*, gallant Lakshman in his red blood fainting fell,

Wrathful Rama saw the combat and arose in godlike might,
Bleeding Ravan turned to Lanka, sought his safety in his flight.

IV

Fall of Kumbha-karna

Once more healed and strong and valiant, Lakshman in his arms
arose,
Safe behind the gates of Lanka humbled Ravan shunned his foes,

Till the stalwart Kumbha-karna from his wonted slumbers woke,
Mightiest he of all the Rakshas;—Ravan thus unto him spoke:

"Thou alone, O Kumbha-karna, can the Raksha's honour save,
Strongest of the Raksha warriors, stoutest-hearted midst the brave,

Speed thee like the Dread Destroyer to the dark and dubious fray,
Cleave through Rama's girdling forces, chase the scattered foe
away!"

Like a mountain's beetling turret Kumbha-karna stout and tall,
Passed the city's lofty portals and the city's girdling wall,

And he raised his voice in battle, sent his cry from shore to shore,
Solid mountains shook and trembled and the sea returned the
roar!

INDRA nor the great VARUNA equalled Kumbha-karna's might,
Vanars trembled at the warrior, sought their safety in their flight,

But the prince of fair Kishkindha, Angad chief of warlike fame,
Marked his panic-stricken forces with a princely warrior's shame.

"Whither fly, ye trembling Vanars?" thus the angry chieftain cried,
"All forgetful of your duty, of your worth and warlike pride,

Deem not stalwart Kumbha-karna is our match in open fight,
Forward let us meet in battle, let us crush his giant might!"

Rallied thus, the broken army stone and tree and massive rock,
Hurled upon the giant Raksha speeding with the lightning's shock,

Vain each flying rock and missile, vain each stout and sturdy
stroke,
On the Raksha's limbs of iron stone and tree in splinters broke.

Dashing through the scattered forces Kumbha-karna fearless stood,
As a forest conflagration feasts upon the parchéd wood,

Far as confines of the ocean, to the causeway they had made,
To the woods or caves or billows, Vanars in their terror fled!

Hanuman of dauntless valour turned not in his fear nor fled,
Heaved a rock with mighty effort on the Raksha's towering head,

With his spear-head Kumbha-karna dashed the flying rock aside,
By the Raksha's weapon stricken Hanuman fell in his pride.

Next Rishabha and brave Nila and the bold Sarabha came,
Gavaksha and Gandha-madan, chieftains of a deathless fame,

But the spear of Kumbha-karna hurled to earth his feeble foes,
Dreadful was the field of carnage, loud the cry of battle rose!

Angad prince of fair Kishkindha, filled with anger and with shame,
Tore a rock with wrathful prowess, to the fatal combat came,

Short the combat, soon the Raksha caught and turned his foe around,
Hurled him in his deathful fury, bleeding, senseless on the ground!

Last, Sugriva king of Vanars with a vengeful anger woke,
Tore a rock from bed of mountain and in proud defiance spoke,

Vain Sugriva's toil and struggle, Kumbha-karna hurled a rock,
Fell Sugriva crushed and senseless 'neath the missile's mighty shock!

Piercing through the Vanar forces, like a flame through forest wood,
Came the Raksha where in glory Lakshman calm and fearless stood,

Short their contest,—Kumbha-karna sought a greater, mightier foe,
To the young and dauntless Lakshman spake in accents soft and low:

"Dauntless prince and matchless warrior, fair Sumitra's gallant son,
Thou hast proved unrivalled prowess and unending glory won,

But I seek a mightier foeman, to thy elder let me go,
I would fight the royal Rama, or to die or slay my foe!"

"*Victor proud!*" *said gallant Lakshman*, "*peerless in thy giant might,*
Conqueror of great Immortals, Lakshman owns thy skill in fight,

Mightier foe than bright Immortals thou shalt meet in fatal war,
Death for thee in guise of Rama tarries yonder, not afar!"

Ill it fared with Kumbha-karna when he strove with Rama's might,
Men on earth nor Gods immortal conquered Rama in the fight,

Deadly arrows keen and flaming from the hero's weapon broke,
Kumbha-karna faint and bleeding felt his death at every stroke,

Last, an arrow pierced his armour, from his shoulders smote his head,
Kumbha-karna, lifeless, headless, rolled upon the gory bed,

Hurled unto the heaving ocean Kumbha-karna's body fell,
And as shaken by a tempest, mighty was the ocean's swell!

V

INDRAJIT'S SACRIFICE AND SECOND BATTLE

Still around beleagured Lanka girdled Rama's living chain,
Raksha chieftain after chieftain strove to break the line in vain,

Sons of Ravan, —brave Narantak was by valiant Angad slain,
Trisiras and fierce Devantak, Hanuman slew on the plain,

Atikaya, tall of stature, was by gallant Lakshman killed,
Ravan wept for slaughtered princes, brave in war in weapons skilled.

"Shed no tears of sorrow, father!" Indrajit exclaimed in pride,
"While thy eldest son surviveth triumph dwells on Ravan's side,

Rama and that stripling Lakshman, I had left them in their gore,
Once again I seek their lifeblood,—they shall live to fight no more.

Hear my vow, O Lord of Rakshas! ere descends yon radiant sun,
Rama's days and gallant Lakshman's on this wide earth shall be done,

Witness INDRA and VIVASWAT, VISHNU great and RUDRA dire,
Witness Sun and Moon and Sadhyas, and the living God of Fire!"

Opened wide the gates of Lanka; in the spacious field of war,
Indrajit arranged his army, foot and horse and battle car,

Then with gifts and sacred *mantras* bent before the God of Fire,
And invoked celestial succour in the battle dread and dire.

With his offerings and his garlands, Indrajit with spices rare,
Worshipped holy VAISWA-NARA on the altar bright and fair,

Spear and mace were ranged in order, dart and bow and shining blade,
Sacred fuel, blood-red garments, fragrant flowers were duly laid,

Head of goat as black as midnight offered then the warrior brave,
And the shooting tongue of red fire omens of a conquest gave,

Curling to the right and smokeless, red and bright as molten gold,
Tongue of flame received the offering of the hero true and bold!

Victory the sign betokens! Bow and dart and shining blade,
Sanctified by holy *mantras*, by the Fire the warrior laid,

Then with weapons consecrated, hid in mists as once before,
Indrajit on helpless foemen did his fatal arrows pour!

Fled the countless Vanar forces, panic-stricken, crushed and slain,
And the dead and dying warriors strewed the gory battle plain,

Then on Rama, and on Lakshman, from his dark and misty shroud,
Indrajit discharged his arrows bright as sunbeams through a cloud.

Scanning earth and bright sky vainly for his dark and hidden foe,
Rama to his brother Lakshman spake in grief and spake in woe:

"Once again that wily Raksha, slaying all our Vanar train,
From his dark and shadowy shelter doth on us his arrows rain,

By the grace of great SWAYAMBHU, Indrajit is lost to sight,
Useless is our human weapon 'gainst his gift of magic might,

If SWAYAMBHU wills it, Lakshman, we shall face these fatal darts,
We shall stand with dauntless patience, we shall die with dauntless
hearts!"

Weaponless but calm and valiant, from the foeman's dart and spell
Patiently the princes suffered, fearlessly the heroes fell!

VI

INDRAJIT'S THIRD BATTLE AND FALL

Healing herbs from distant mountains Hanuman in safety brought,
Rama rose and gallant Lakshman, once again their foemen sought,

And when night its sable mantle o'er the earth and ocean drew,
Forcing through the gates of Lanka to the frightened city flew!

Gallant sons of Kumbha-karna vainly fought to stem the tide,
Hanuman and brave Sugriva slew the brothers in their pride,

Makaraksha, shark-eyed warrior, vainly struggled with the foe,
Rama laid him pierced and lifeless by an arrow from his bow.

Indrajit arose in anger for his gallant kinsmen slayed,
In his arts and deep devices Sita's beauteous image made,

And he placed the form of beauty on his speeding battle car,
With his sword he smote the image in the gory field of war!

Rama heard the fatal message which his faithful Vanars gave,
And a deathlike trance and tremor fell upon the warrior brave,

But Bibhishan deep in wisdom to the anguished Rama came,
With his words of consolation spake of Rama's righteous dame:

"Trust me, Rama, trust thy comrade,—for I know our wily house,—
Indrajit slays not the woman whom his father seeks as spouse,

'Tis for Sita, impious Ravan meets thee on the battle-field,
Stakes his life and throne and empire, but thy Sita will not yield,

Deem not that the king of Rakshas will permit her blood be shed,
Indrajit slays not the woman whom his father seeks to wed!

'Twas an image of thy Sita, Indrajit hath cleft in twain,
While our army wails and sorrows,—he performs his rites again,

To the holy Nikumbhila, Indrajit in secret hies,
For the rites which yield him prowess, hide him in the cloudy skies.

Let young Lakshman seek the foeman ere his magic rites be done,—
Once the sacrifice completed, none can combat Ravan's son,—

Let young Lakshman speed through Lanka till his wily foe is found,
Slay the secret sacrificer on the sacrificial ground!"

Unto holy Nikumbhila, Lakshman with Bibhishan went,
Bravest, choicest of the army, Rama with his brother sent,

Magic rites and sacrifices Indrajit had scarce begun,
When surprised by armèd foemen rose in anger Ravan's son!

"Art thou he," thus to Bibhishan, Indrajit in anger spake,
"Brother of my royal father, stealing thus my life to take,

Raksha, born of Raksha parents, dost thou glory in this deed,
Traitor to thy king and kinsmen, false to us in direst need?

Scorn and pity fill my bosom thus to see thee leave thy kin,
Serving as a slave of foemen, stooping to a deed of sin,

For the slave who leaves his kindred, basely seeks the foeman's
grace,
Meets destruction from the foeman after he destroys his race!"

"Untaught child of impure passions," thus Bibhishan answer made,
"Of my righteous worth unconscious bitter accents hast thou said,

Know, proud youth, that Truth and Virtue in my heart precedence
take,
And we shun the impious kinsman as we shun the pois'nous snake!

Listen youth! this earth no longer bears thy father's sin and strife,
Plunder of the righteous neighbour, passion for the neighbour's wife,

Earth and skies have doomed thy father for his sin-polluted reign,
Unto Gods his proud defiance and his wrongs to sons of men!

Listen more! this fated Lanka groans beneath her load of crime,
And shall perish in her folly by the ruthless hand of Time,

Thou shalt perish and thy father and this proud presumptuous state,
Lakshman meets thee, impious Rakshas, by the stern decree of Fate!"

"Hast thou too forgot the lesson," Indrajit to Lakshman said,
"Twice in field of war unconscious thee with Rama have I laid,

Dost thou stealing like a serpent brave my yet unconquered might,
Perish, boy, in thy presumption, in this last and fatal fight!"

Spake the hero: "Like a coward hid beneath a mantling cloud,
Thou hast battled like a caitiff safe behind thy sheltering shroud,

Now I seek an open combat, time is none to prate or speak,
Boastful word is coward's weapon, weapons and thy arrows seek!"

Soon they mixed in dubious combat, fury fired each foeman's heart,
Either warrior felt his rival worthy of his bow and dart,

Lakshman with his hurtling arrows pierced the Raksha's golden mail,
Shattered by the Raksha's weapons Lakshman's useless armour fell,

Red with gore and dim in eyesight still the chiefs in fury fought,
Neither quailed before his foeman, pause nor grace nor mercy sought,

Till with more than human valour Lakshman drew his bow amain,
Slayed the Raksha's steeds and driver, severed too his bow in twain.

"If the great and godlike Rama is in faith and duty true,
Gods assist the cause of virtue !"—Lakshman uttered as he drew,

Fatal was the dart unerring,—Gods assist the true and bold,—
On the field of Nikumbhila, Lakshman's foeman headless rolled !

VII

Ravan's Lament

"Quenched the light of Rakshas' valour !" so the message-bearer said,
"Lakshman with the deep Bibhishan hath thy son in battle slayed,

Fallen is our prince and hero and his day on earth is done,
In a brighter world, O monarch, lives thy brave thy gallant son !"

Anguish filled the father's bosom and his fleeting senses failed,
Till to deeper sorrow wakened Lanka's monarch wept and wailed :

"Greatest of my gallant warriors, dearest to thy father's heart,
Victor over bright Immortals,—art thou slain by Lakshman's dart,

Noble prince whose peerless arrows could the peaks of Mandar stain,
And could daunt the Dread Destroyer,—art thou by a mortal slain?

But thy valour lends a radiance to elysium's sunny clime,
And thy bright name adds a lustre to the glorious rolls of time,

In the skies the bright Immortals lisp thy name with terror pale,
On the earth our maids and matrons mourn thy fall with piercing wail!

Hark! the voice of lamentation waking in the palace halls,
Like the voice of woe in forests when the forest monarch falls,

Hark! the wailing widowed princess, mother weeping for her son,
Leaving them in tears and anguish, Indrajit, where art thou gone?

Full of years,—so oft I pondered,—when the monarch Ravan dies,
Indrajit shall watch his bedside, Indrajit shall close his eyes,

But the course of nature changes, and the father weeps the son,
Youth is fallen, and the aged lives to fight the foe alone!"

Tears of sorrow, slow and silent, fell upon the monarch's breast,
Then a swelling rage and passion woke within his heaving chest,

Like the sun of scorching summer glowed his face in wrathful shame,
From his brow and rolling eyeballs issued sparks of living flame!

"Perish she!" exclaimed the monarch, "she-wolf Sita dies to-day,
Indrajit but cleft her image, Ravan will the woman slay!"

Followed by his trembling courtiers, regal robes and garments rent,
Ravan shaking in his passion to *Asoka's* garden went,

Maddened by his wrath and anguish, with his drawn and flaming sword,
Sought the shades where soft-eyed Sita silent sorrowed for her lord.

Woman's blood the royal sabre on that fatal day had stained,
But his true and faithful courtiers Ravan's wrathful hand restrained,

And the watchful Raksha females girdled round the sorrowing dame,
Flung them on the path of Ravan to withstand a deed of shame.

"Not against a woman, Ravan, mighty warriors raise their hand,
In the battle," spake the courtiers, "duty bids thee use thy brand,

Versed in *Vedas* and in learning, court not thus a caitiff's fate,
Woman's blood pollutes our valour, closes heaven's eternal gate!

Leave the woman in her sorrow, mount upon thy battle car,
Faithful to our king and leader we will wake the voice of war,

'Tis the fourteenth day auspicious of the dark and waning moon,
Glory waiteth thee in battle and thy vengeance cometh soon,

All-resistless in the contest slay thy foeman in his pride,
Seek as victor of the combat widowed Sita as thy bride!"

Slow and sullen, dark and silent, Ravan then his wrath restrained,
Vengeance on his son's destroyer deep within his bosom reigned!

VIII

Ravan's Second Battle and Vengeance

Voice of woe and lamentation and the cry of woman's wail,
Issuing from the homes of Lanka did the monarch's ears assail,

And a mighty thought of vengeance waked within the monarch's
heart,
And he heaved a sigh of anguish as he grasped his bow and dart:

"Arm each chief and gallant Raksha! be our sacred duty done,
Ravan seeks a fitting vengeance for his brave and noble son,

Mahodar and Virupaksha, Mahaparshwa warrior tall,
Arm! this fated day will witness Lakshman's or your monarch's fall!

Call to mind each slaughtered hero,—Khara, Dushan, slain in fight,
Kumbha-karna giant warrior, Indrajit of magic might,

Earth nor sky shall hide my foemen nor the ocean's heaving swell,
Scattered ranks of Rama's forces shall my speedy vengeance tell,

Be the red-earth strewn and covered with our countless foemen slain,
Hungry wolves and blood-beaked vultures feed upon the ghastly
plain,

For his great and gallant brother, for his brave and beauteous son,
Ravan seeks a fitting vengeance, Rakshas be your duty done!"

House to house, in Lanka's city, Ravan's royal hest was heard,
Street and lane poured forth their warriors by a mighty passion stirred,

With their javelin and sabre, mace and club and axe and pike,
Sataghni and *bhindipala*, quoit and discus quick to strike.

And they formed the line of tuskers and the line of battle car,
Mule and camel fit for burden and the fiery steed of war,

Serried ranks of armèd soldiers shook the earth beneath their tread,
Horsemen that on wings of lightning o'er the field of battle spread,

Drum and conch and sounding trumpet waked the echoes of the sky,
Pataha and loud *mridanga* and the people's maddening cry,

Thundering through the gates of Lanka, Ravan's lofty chariot passed,
Destined by his fortune, Ravan ne'er again those portals crost!

And the sun was dim and clouded and a sudden darkness fell,
Birds gave forth their boding voices and the earth confessed a spell,

Gouts of blood in rain descended, startled coursers turned to fly,
Vultures swooped upon the banner, jackals yelled their doleful cry,

Omens of a dark disaster mantled o'er the vale and rock,
And the ocean heaved in billows, nations felt the earthquake's shock!

Darkly closed the fatal battle, sturdy Vanars fell in fight,
Warlike leaders of the Rakshas perished neath the foeman's might,

Mahodhar and Virupaksha were by bold Sugriva slain,
Crushed by Angad, Mahaparshwa slumbered lifeless on the plain,

But with more than mortal valour Ravan swept the ranks of war,
Warriors fell beneath his prowess, fled before his mighty car,

Cleaving through the Vanar forces, filled with vengeance deep and dire,
Ravan marked the gallant Lakshman flaming like a crimson fire!

Like the tempest cloud of summer Ravan's wingéd coursers flew,
But Bibhishan in his prowess soon the gallant chargers slew,

Dashing from his useless chariot Ravan leaped upon the ground,
And his false and traitor brother by his dearest foeman found!

Wrathful Ravan marked Bibhishan battling by the foeman's side
And he hurled his pond'rous weapon for to slay him in his pride,

Lakshman marked the mighty jav'lin as it winged its whizzing flight,
Cleft it in its onward passage, saved Bibhishan by his might!

Grimly smiled the angry Ravan gloating in his vengeful wrath,
Spake to young and dauntless Lakshman daring thus to cross his path:

"Welcome, Lakshman! thee I battle for thy deed of darkness done,
Face the anger of a father, cruel slayer of the son,

By thy skill and by thy valour, false Bibhishan thou hast saved,
Save thyself! Deep in this bosom is a cruel grief engraved!"

Father's grief and sad remembrance urged the lightning-wingéd dart,
Ravan's *Sakti* fell resistless on the senseless Lakshman's heart,

Wrathful Rama saw the combat and arose in godlike might,
Carless, steedless, wounded Ravan sought his safety in his flight.

IX

Rama's Lament

"Art thou fallen," sorrowed Rama, "weary of this endless strife,
Lakshman, if thy days are ended, Rama recks not for his life,

Gone is Rama's wonted valour, weapons leave his nerveless hand,
Drop his bow and shining arrows, useless hangs his sheathéd brand!

Art thou fallen, gallant Lakshman, death and faintness on me creep,
Weary of this fatal contest let me by my brother sleep,

Weary of the strife and triumph, since my faithful friend is gone,
Rama follows in his footsteps and his task on earth is done!

Thou hast from the far Ayodhya, followed me in deepest wood,
In the thickest of the battle thou hast by thy elder stood,

Love of woman, love of comrade, trite is love of kith and kind,
Love like thine, true-hearted brother, not on earth we often find!

When Sumitra seeks thee, Lakshman, ever weeping for thy sake,
When she asks me of her hero, what reply shall Rama make,

What reply, when Bharat questions,—Where is he who went to wood,
Where is true and faithful Lakshman who beside his elder stood?

What great crime or fatal shadow darkens o'er my hapless life,
Victim to the sins of Rama sinless Lakshman falls in strife,

Best of brothers, best of warriors, wherefore thus unconscious lie,
Mother, wife, and brother wait thee, ope once more thy sleeping eye!"

Tara's father, wise Susena, gentle consolation lent,
Hanuman from distant mountains herbs of healing virtue rent,

And by loving Rama tended, Lakshman in his strength arose,
Stirred by thoughts of fatal vengeance Rama sought the flying foes.

X

Celestial Arms and Chariot

Not in dastard terror Ravan sought his safety in his flight,
But to seek fresh steeds of battle ere he faced his foeman's might,

Harnessing his gallant coursers to a new and glorious car,
Sunlike in its radiant splendour, Ravan came once more to war.

Gods in wonder watched the contest of the more than mortal foes,
Ravan mighty in his vengeance, Rama lofty in his woes,

Gods in wonder marked the heroes, lion-like in jungle wood,
INDRA sent his arms and chariot where the human warrior stood!

"*Speed, Matali,*" *thus spake* INDRA, "*speed thee with my heavenly car,*
Where on foot the righteous Rama meets his mounted foe in war,

Speed, for Ravan's days are ended, and his moments brief and few,
Rama strives for right and virtue,—Gods assist the brave and true!"

Brave Matali drove the chariot drawn by steeds like solar ray,
Where the true and righteous Rama sought his foe in fatal fray,

Shining arms and heavenly weapons he to lofty Rama gave,—
When the righteous strive and struggle, Gods assist the true and brave!

"Take this car," so said Matali, "which the helping Gods provide,
Rama, take these steeds celestial, INDRA's golden chariot ride,

Take this royal bow and quiver, wear this falchion dread and dire,
VISWA-KARMAN forged this armour in the flames of heavenly fire,

I shall be thy chariot driver and shall speed the thund'ring car,
Slay the sin-polluted Ravan in this last and fatal war!"

Rama mounted on the chariot clad in arms of heavenly sheen,
And he mingled in a contest mortal eyes have never seen!

XI

RAVAN'S THIRD BATTLE AND FALL

Gods and mortals watched the contest and the heroes of the war,
Ravan speeding on his chariot, Rama on the heavenly car,

And a fiercer form the warriors in their fiery frenzy wore,
And a deeper weight of hatred on their anguished bosoms bore,

Clouds of dread and deathful arrows hid the radiant face of sky,
Darker grew the day of combat, fiercer grew the contest high!

Pierced by Ravan's pointed weapons bleeding Rama owned no pain,
Rama's arrows keen and piercing sought his foeman's life in vain,

Long the dubious battle lasted, and with wilder fury fraught,
Wounded, faint, and still unyielding, blind with wrath the rivals fought,

Pike and club and mace and trident scaped from Ravan's vengeful hand,
Spear and arrows Rama wielded, and his bright and flaming brand!

Long the dubious battle lasted, shook the ocean, hill and dale,
Winds were hushed in voiceless terror and the livid sun was pale,

Still the dubious battle lasted, until Rama in his ire,
Wielded BRAHMA's deathful weapon flaming with celestial fire!

Weapon which the Saint Agastya had unto the hero given,
Winged as lightning dart of INDRA, fatal as the bolt of heaven,

Wrapped in smoke and flaming flashes, speeding from the circled bow,
Pierced the iron heart of Ravan, lain the lifeless hero low,

And a cry of pain and terror from the Raksha ranks arose,
And a shout from joying Vanars as they smote their fleeing foes!

Heavenly flowers in rain descended on the red and gory plain,
And from unseen harps and timbrels rose a soft celestial strain,

And the ocean heaved in gladness, brighter shone the sunlit sky,
Soft and cool the gentle zephyrs through the forest murmured by,

Sweetest scent and fragrant odours wafted from celestial trees,
Fell upon the earth and ocean, rode upon the laden breeze!

Voice of blessing from the bright sky fell on Raghus' valiant son,—
"Champion of the true and righteous! now thy noble task is done!"

XII

MANDODARI'S LAMENT AND THE FUNERALS

"Hast thou fallen," wept in anguish Ravan's first and eldest bride,
Mandodari, slender-waisted, Queen of Lanka's state and pride,

"Hast thou fallen, king and consort, more than Gods in warlike might,
Slain by man, whom bright Immortals feared to face in dubious fight?

Not a man!—the Dark Destroyer came to thee in mortal form,
Or the heaven-traversing VISHNU, INDRA ruler of the storm,

Gods of sky in shape of Vanars helped the dark and cruel deed,
Girdling round the Discus-Wielder in the battle's direst need!

Well I knew,—when Khara, Dushan ,were by Rama's prowess slain,
Rama was no earthly mortal, he who crossed the mighty main,

Well I knew,—when with his army he invested Lanka's gate,
Rama was no earthly mortal but the messenger of Fate,

And I prayed,—the faithful Sita might unto her consort go,
For 'tis writ that nations perish for a righteous woman's woe,

But for impious lust of woman,—all forgetful of thy wife,
Thou hast lost thy crown and kingdom, thou hast lost thy fated life!

Woe to me! the sad remembrance haunts my tortured bosom still,
Of our days on famed Kailasa or on Meru's golden hill,

Gone the days of joy and gladness, Mandodari's days are done,
Since her lord and king and husband from her dear embrace is gone!"

Sorely wept the Queen of Lanka; Rama, tender, tearful, true,
Bade the funeral rites and honours to a fallen foeman due,

And they heaped the wood of *Chandan* and the fragrant garland laid,
On the pyre they lifted Ravan in the richest robes arrayed,

Weeping queens and sorrowing Rakshas round their fallen leader stood,
Brahmans with their chaunted *mantras* piled the dry and scented wood,

Oil and cords and sacred offerings were upon the altar laid,
And a goat of inky darkness as a sacrifice was slayed.

Piously the good Bibhishan lighted Ravan's funeral pyre,
And the zephyrs gently blowing fanned the bright and blazing fire,

Slow and sad with due ablutions mourners left the funeral site,
Rama then unstrung his weapon, laid aside his arms of might.

BOOK XI

RAJYA-ABHISHEKA

(Rama's Return and Consecration)

The real Epic ends with the war, and with Rama's happy return to Ayodhya. Sita proves her stainless virtue by an Ordeal of Fire, and returns with her lord and with Lakshman in an aërial car, which Ravan had won from the Gods, and which Bibhishan made over to Rama. Indian poets are never tired of descriptions of nature, and the poet of the Ramayana takes advantage of Rama's journey from Ceylon to Oudh to give us a bird's-eye view of the whole continent of India, as well as to recapitulate the principal incidents of his great Epic.

The gathering of men at Ayodhya, the greetings to Rama, and his consecration by the Vedic bard Vasishtha, are among the most pleasing passages in the whole poem. And the happiness enjoyed by men during the reign of Rama—described in the last few couplets of this Book—is an article of belief and a living tradition in India to this day.

The portions translated in this Book form the whole or portions of Sections cxviii., cxx., cxxv., cxxix., and cxxx., of Book vi. of the original text.

I.

Ordeal by Fire

For she dwelt in Ravan's dwelling,—rumour clouds a woman's fame—
Righteous Rama's brow was clouded, saintly Sita spake in shame :

"Wherefore spake ye not, my Rama, if your bosom doubts my faith,
Dearer than a dark suspicion to a woman were her death !

Wherefore, Rama, with your token came your vassal o'er the wave,
To assist a fallen woman and a tainted wife to save,

Wherefore with your mighty forces crossed the ocean in your pride,
Risked your life in endless combats for a sin-polluted bride?

Hast thou, Rama, all forgotten?—Saintly Janak saw my birth,
Child of harvest-bearing furrow, Sita sprang from Mother Earth,

As a maiden true and stainless unto thee I gave my hand,
As a consort fond and faithful roved with thee from land to land!

But a woman pleadeth vainly when suspicion clouds her name,
Lakshman, if thou lov'st thy sister, light for me the funeral flame,

When the shadow of dishonour darkens o'er a woman's life,
Death alone is friend and refuge of a true and trustful wife,

When a righteous lord and husband turns his cold averted eyes,
Funeral flame dispels suspicion, honour lives when woman dies!"

Dark was Rama's gloomy visage and his lips were firmly sealed,
And his eye betrayed no weakness, word disclosed no thought concealed,

Silent heaved his heart in anguish, silent drooped his tortured head,
Lakshman with a throbbing bosom funeral pyre for Sita made,

And Videha's sinless daughter prayed unto the Gods above,
On her lord and wedded consort cast her dying looks of love!

"*If in act and thought,*" *she uttered*, "*I am true unto my name,*
Witness of our sins and virtues, may this Fire protect my fame!

If a false and lying scandal brings a faithful woman shame,
Witness of our sins and virtues, may this Fire protect my fame!

If in life-long loving duty I am free from sin and blame,
Witness of our sins and virtues, may this Fire protect my fame!"

Fearless in her faith and valour Sita stepped upon the pyre,
And her form of beauty vanished circled by the clasping fire,

And an anguish shook the people like the ocean tempest-tost,
Old and young and maid and matron wept for Sita true and lost,

For bedecked in golden splendour and in gems and rich attire,
Sita vanished in the red fire of the newly lighted pyre!

Rishis and the great *Gandharvas*, Gods who know each secret deed,
Witnessed Sita's high devotion and a woman's lofty creed,

And the earth by ocean girdled with its wealth of teeming life,
Witnessed deed of dauntless duty of a true and stainless wife!

II

Woman's Truth Vindicated

Slow the red flames rolled asunder, God of Fire incarnate came,
Holding in his radiant bosom fair Videha's sinless dame,

Not a curl upon her tresses, not a blossom on her brow,
Not a fibre of her mantle did with tarnished lustre glow!

Witness of our sins and virtues, God of Fire incarnate spake,
Bade the sorrow-stricken Rama back his sinless wife to take:

"Ravan in his impious folly forced from thee thy faithful dame,
Guarded by her changeless virtue, Sita still remains the same,

Tempted oft by female Rakshas in the dark and dismal wood,
In her woe and in her sadness true to thee hath Sita stood,

Courted oft by royal Ravan in the forest far and lone,
True to wedded troth and virtue Sita thought of thee alone,

Pure is she in thought and action, pure and stainless, true and meek,
I, the witness of all actions, thus my sacred mandate speak!"

Rama's forehead was unclouded and a radiance lit his eye,
And his bosom heaved in gladness as he spake in accents high:

"Never from the time I saw her in her maiden days of youth,
Have I doubted Sita's virtue, Sita's fixed and changeless truth,

I have known her ever sinless,—let the world her virtue know,
For the God of Fire is witness to her truth and changeless vow!

Ravan in his pride and passion conquered not a woman's love,
For the virtuous like the bright fire in their native radiance move,

Ravan in his rage and folly conquered not a faithful wife,
For like ray of sun unsullied is a righteous woman's life,

Be the wide world now a witness,—pure and stainless is my dame,
Rama shall not leave his consort till he leaves his righteous fame!"

In his tears the contrite Rama clasped her in a soft embrace,
And the fond forgiving Sita in his bosom hid her face!

III

Return Home by the Aerial Car

"Mark my love," so Rama uttered, as on flying Pushpa car,
Borne by swans, the home-returning exiles left the field of war,

"Lanka's proud and castled city on Trikuta's triple crest,
As on peaks of bold Kailasa mansions of Immortals rest!

Mark the gory fields surrounding where the Vanars in their might,
Faced and fought the charging Rakshas in the long and deathful fight,

Indrajit and Kumbha-karna, Ravan and his chieftains slain,
Fell upon the field of battle and their red blood soaks the plain.

Mark where dark-eyed Mandodari, Ravan's slender-waisted wife,
Wept her widow's tears of anguish when her monarch lost his life,

She hath dried her tears of sorrow and bestowed her heart and hand,
On Bibhishan good and faithful, crowned king of Lanka's land.

See my love, round Ceylon's island how the ocean billows roar,
Hiding pearls in caves of corals, strewing shells upon the shore,

And the causeway far-extending,—monument of Rama's fame,—
'Rama's Bridge' to distant ages shall our deathless deeds proclaim!

See the rockbound fair Kishkindha and her mountain-girdled town,
Where I slayed the warrior Bali, placed Sugriva on the throne,

And the hill of Rishyamuka where Sugriva first I met,
Gave him word,—he would be monarch ere the evening's sun had set.

See the sacred lake of Pampa by whose wild and echoing shore,
Rama poured his lamentations when he saw his wife no more,

And the woods of Janasthana where Jatayu fought and bled,
When the deep deceitful Ravan with my trusting Sita fled.

Dost thou mark, my soft-eyed Sita, cottage on the river's shore,
Where in righteous peace and penance Sita lived in days of yore,

And by gloomy Godavari, Saint Agastya's home of love,
Holy men by holy duties sanctify the sacred grove!

Dost thou, o'er the Dandak forest, view the Chitrakuta hill,
Deathless bard the Saint Valmiki haunts its shade and crystal rill,

Thither came the righteous Bharat and my loving mother came,
Longing in their hearts to take us to Ayodhya's town of fame.

Dost thou, dear devoted Sita, see the Jumna in her might,
Where in Bharad-waja's *asram* passed we, love, a happy night,

And the broad and ruddy Ganga sweeping in her regal pride,
Forest-dweller faithful Guha crossed us to the southern side.

Joy! joy! my gentle Sita! Fair Ayodhya looms above,
Ancient seat of Raghu's empire, nest of Rama's hope and love,.

Bow, bow, to bright Ayodhya! Darksome did the exiles roam,
Now their weary toil is ended in their father's ancient home!"

IV

GREETINGS

Message from returning Rama, Vanars to Ayodhya brought,
Righteous Bharat gave his mandate with a holy joy distraught:

"Let our city shrines and *chaityas* with a lofty music shake,
And our priests to bright Immortals grateful gifts and offerings
make,

Bards, reciters of *Puranas*, minstrels versed in ancient song,
Women with their tuneful voices lays of sacred love prolong,

Let our queens and stately courtiers step in splendour and in state,
Chieftains with their marshalled forces range along the city gate,

And our white-robed holy Brahmans, hymns and sacred *mantras*
sing,
Offer greetings to our brother, render homage to our king!"

Brave Satrughna heard his elder and his mandate duly kept:
"Be our great and sacred city levelled, cleansed, and duly swept,

And the grateful earth be sprinkled with the water from the well,
Strewn with parchéd rice and offering and with flower of sweetest
smell,

On each turret tower and temple let our flags and colours wave,
On the gates of proud Ayodhya plant Ayodhya's banners brave,

Gay festoons of flowering creeper home and street and dwelling
line,
And in gold and glittering garment let the gladdened city shine!"

Elephants in golden trappings thousand chiefs and nobles bore,
Chariots cars and gallant chargers speeding by Sarayu's shore,

And the serried troops of battle marched with colours rich and
brave,
Proudly o'er the gay procession did Ayodhya's banners wave.

In their stately gilded litters royal dames and damsels came,
Queen Kausalya first and foremost, Queen Sumitra rich in fame,

Pious priest and learned Brahman, chief of guild from near and far,
Noble chief and stately courtier with the wreath and water jar.

Girt by minstrel bard and herald chanting glorious deeds of yore,
Bharat came,—his elder's sandals still the faithful younger bore,—

Silver-white his proud umbrella, silver-white his garland brave,
Silver-white the fan of *chowri* which his faithful henchmen wave.

Stately march of gallant chargers and the roll of battle car,
Heavy tread of royal tuskers and the beat of drum of war,

Dundubhi and echoing *sankha*, voice of nations gathered nigh,
Shook the city's tower and temple and the pealing vault of sky!

Sailing o'er the cloudless ether Rama's Pushpa chariot came,
And ten-thousand jocund voices shouted Rama's joyous name,

Women with their loving greetings, children with their joyous cry,
Tottering age and lisping infant hailed the righteous chief and high.

Bharat lifted up his glances unto Rama from afar,
Unto Sita, unto Lakshman, seated on the Pushpa car,

And he wafted high his greetings and he poured his pious lay,
As one wafts the chaunted *mantra* to the rising God of Day!

Silver swans by Rama's bidding soft descended from the air,
And on earth the chariot lighted,—car of flowers divinely fair,—

Bharat mounting on the chariot, sought his long-lost elder's grace,
Rama held his faithful younger in a brother's dear embrace.

With his greetings unto Lakshman, unto Rama's faithful dame,
To Bibhishan and Sugriva and each chief who thither came,

Bharat took the jewelled sandals with the rarest gems inlaid,
Placed them at the feet of Rama and in humble accents said:

"Tokens of thy rule and empire, *these* have filled thy royal throne,
Faithful to his trust and duty Bharat renders back thine own,

Bharat's life is joy and gladness, for returned from distant shore,
Thou shalt rule thy spacious kingdom and thy loyal men once more,

Thou shalt hold thy rightful empire and assume thy royal crown,
Faithful to his trust and duty,—Bharat renders back thine own!"

V

The Consecration

Joy! joy! in bright Ayodhya gladness filled the hearts of all,
Joy! joy! a lofty music sounded in the royal hall,

Fourteen years of woe were ended, Rama now assumed his own,
And they placed the weary wand'rer on his father's ancient throne,

And they brought the sacred water from each distant stream and hill,
From the vast and boundless ocean, from each far and sacred rill.

Vasishtha the Bard of *Vedas* with auspicious rites and meet,
Placed the monarch and his consort on the gemmed and jewelled
 seat,

Gautama and Katyayana, Vamadeva priest of yore,
Jabali and wise Vijaya versed in holy ancient lore,

Poured the fresh and fragrant water on the consecrated king,
As the Gods anointed INDRA from the pure ethereal spring!

Vedic priests with sacred *mantra*, dark-eyed virgins with their song,
Warriors girt in arms and weapons round the crownéd monarch
 throng,

Juices from each fragrant creeper on his royal brow they place,
And his father's crown and jewels Rama's ample forehead grace,

And as Manu, first of monarchs, was enthroned in days of yore,
So was Rama consecrated by the priests of Vedic lore!

Brave Satrughna on his brother cast the white umbrella's shade,
Bold Sugriva and Bibhishan waved the *chowri* gem-inlaid,

VAYU, God of gentle zephyrs, gift of golden garland lent,
INDRA, God of rain and sunshine, wreath of pearls to Rama sent,

Gay *Gandharvas* raised the music, fair *Apsaras* formed the ring,
Men in nations hailed their Rama as their lord and righteous king!

And 'tis told by ancient sages, during Rama's happy reign,
Death untimely, dire diseases, came not to his subject men,

Widows wept not in their sorrow for their lords untimely lost,
Mothers wailed not in their anguish for their babes by YAMA *crost,*

Robbers, cheats, and gay deceivers tempted not with lying word,
Neighbour loved his righteous neighbour and the people loved their lord!

Trees their ample produce yielded as returning seasons went,
And the earth in grateful gladness never failing harvest lent,

Rains descended in their season, never came the blighting gale,
Rich in crop and rich in pasture was each soft and smiling vale,

Loom and anvil gave their produce and the tilled and fertile soil,
And the nation lived rejoicing in their old ancestral toil!

BOOK XII

ASWA-MEDHA

(*Sacrifice of the Horse*)

The real Epic ends with Rama's happy return to Ayodhya. An *Uttara-Kanda* or Supplement is added, describing the fate of Sita, and giving the poem a sad ending.

The dark cloud of suspicion still hung on the fame of Sita, and the people of Ayodhya made reflections on the conduct of their king, who had taken back into his house a woman who had lived in the palace of Ravan. Rama gave way to the opinion of his people and he sent away his loving and faithful Sita to live in forests once more.

Sita found an asylum in the hermitage of Valmiki, the reputed author of this Epic, and there gave birth to twins, Lava and Kusa. Years passed on, and Lava and Kusa grew up as hermit boys, and as pupils of Valmiki.

After years had passed, Rama performed a great Horse-sacrifice. Kings and princes were invited from neighbouring countries, and a great feast was held. Valmiki came to the sacrifice, and his pupils, Lava and Kusa, chanted there the great Epic, the *Ramayana*, describing the deeds of Rama. In this interesting portion of the poem we find how songs and poetry were handed down in ancient India by memory. The boys had learnt the whole of the Epic by heart, and chanted portions of it, day after day, till the recital was completed. We are told that the poem consists of seven books, 500 cantos, and 24,000 couplets. Twenty cantos were recited each day, so that the recital of the whole poem must have taken twenty-five days. It was by such feats of memory and by such recitals that literature was preserved in ancient times in India.

Rama recognised his sons in the boy-minstrels, and his heart yearned once more for Sita whom he had banished, but never forgotten. He asked the Poet Valmiki to restore his wife to him, and he desired that Sita might once more prove her purity in the great assembly, so that he might take her back with the approval of his people.

Sita came. But her life had been darkened by an unjust suspicion, her heart was broken, and she invoked the Earth to take her back. And the Earth, which had given Sita birth, yawned and took back her suffering child into her bosom.

In the ancient hymns of the *Rig Veda*, Sita is simply the goddess of the field-furrow which bears crops for men. We find how that simple conception is concealed in the *Ramayana*, where Sita the heroine of the Epic is still born of the field-furrow, and after all her adventures returns to the earth. To the millions of men and women in India, however, Sita is not an allegory; she lives in their hearts and affections as the model of womanly love, womanly devotion, and a wife's noble self-abnegation.

The portions translated in this Book form the whole or portions of Sections xcii., xciii., xciv., and xcvii., of Book vii. of the original text.

I

The Sacrifice

Years have passed; the lonely Rama in his joyless palace reigned,
And for righteous duty yearning, *Aswa-medha* rite ordained,

And a steed of darkest sable with the valiant Lakshman sent,
And with troops and faithful courtiers to Naimisha's forest went.

Fair was far Naimisha's forest by the limpid Gumti's shore,
Monarchs came and warlike chieftains. Brahmans versed in sacred lore,

Bharat with each friend and kinsman served them with the choicest food,
Proud retainers by each chieftain and each crownéd monarch stood.

Palaces and stately mansions were for royal guests assigned,
Peaceful homes for learned Brahmans were with trees umbrageous lined,

Gifts were made unto the needy, cloth by skilful weavers wrought,
Ere the suppliants spake their wishes, ere they shaped their inmost
thought!

Rice unto the helpless widow, to the orphan wealth and gold,
Gifts they gave to holy Brahmans, shelter to the weak and old,

Garments to the grateful people crowding by their monarch's door,
Food and drink unto the hungry, home unto the orphan poor.

Ancient *rishis* had not witnessed feast like this in any land,
Bright Immortals in their bounty blest not with a kinder hand,

Through the year and circling seasons lasted Rama's sacred feast,
And the untold wealth of Rama by his kindly gifts increased!

II

Valmiki and His Pupils

Foremost midst the gathered Sages to the holy *yajna* came
Deathless Bard of Lay Immortal—Saint Valmiki rich in fame,

Midst the humble homes of *rishis*, on the confines of the wood,
Cottage of the Saint Valmiki in the shady garden stood.

Fruits and berries from the jungle, water from the crystal spring,
With a careful hand Valmiki did unto his cottage bring,

And he spake to gentle Lava, Kusa child of righteous fame,—
Sita's sons, as youthful hermits to the sacred feast they came:

"Lift your voices, righteous pupils, and your richest music lend,
Sing the Lay of *Ramayana* from the first unto the end,

Sing it to the holy Brahman, to the warrior fair and tall,
In the crowded street and pathway, in the monarch's palace hall,

Sing it by the door of Rama,—he ordains this mighty feast,
Sing it to the royal ladies,—they shall to the story list,

Sing from day to day unwearied, in this sacrificial site,
Chant to all the gathered nations Rama's deeds of matchless might,

And this store of fruits and berries will allay your thirst and toil,
Gentle children of the forest, unknown strangers in this soil!

Twenty cantos of the Epic, morn to night, recite each day,
Till from end to end is chanted *Ramayana's* deathless Lay,

Ask no alms, receive no riches, nor of your misfortunes tell,
Useless unto us is bounty who in darksome forests dwell,

Children of the wood and mountain, cruel fortune clouds your birth,
Stainless virtue be your shelter, virtue be your wealth on earth!

If the royal Rama questions and your lineage seeks to know,
Say,—Valmiki is our Teacher and our Sire on earth below,

Wake your harps to notes of rapture and your softest accents lend,
With the music of the poet music of your voices blend,

Bow unto the mighty monarch, bow to Rama fair and tall,
He is father of his subjects, he is lord of creatures all!"

III

Recital of the Ramayana

When the silent night was ended, and their pure ablutions done,
Joyous went the minstrel brothers, and their lofty lay begun,

Rama to the hermit minstrels lent a monarch's willing ear,
Blended with the simple music dulcet was the lay to hear,

And so sweet the chanted accents, Rama's inmost soul was stirred,
With his royal guests and courtiers still the deathless lay he heard!

Heralds versed in old *Puranas*, Brahmans skilled in pious rite,
Minstrels deep in lore of music, poets fired by heavenly might,

Watchers of the constellations, min'sters of the festive day,
Men of science and of logic, bards who sang the ancient lay,

Painters skilled and merry dancers who the festive joy prolong,
Hushed and silent in their wonder listed to the wondrous song!

And as poured the flood of music through the bright and live-
long day,
Eyes and ears and hearts insatiate drank the nectar of the lay,

And the eager people whispered: "See the boys, how like our king,
As two drops of limpid water from the parent bubble spring!

Were the boys no hermit-children, in the hermit's garments clad,
We would deem them Rama's image,—Rama as a youthful lad!"

Twenty cantos of the Epic thus the youthful minstrels sung,
And the voice of stringéd music through the Epic rolled along,

Out spake Rama in his wonder: "Scarce I know who these may be,
Eighteen thousand golden pieces be the children-minstrels' fee!"

"Not so," answered thus the children, "we in darksome forests
dwell,
Gold and silver, bounteous monarch, forest life beseem not well!"

"Noble children!" uttered Rama, "dear to me the words you say,
Tell me who composed this Epic,—Father of this deathless Lay?"

"*Saint Valmiki,*" *spake the minstrels,* "*framed the great immortal song,
Four and twenty thousand verses to this noble Lay belong,*

*Untold tales of deathless virtue sanctify his sacred line,
And five hundred glorious cantos in this glorious Epic shine,*

*In six Books of mighty splendour was the poet's task begun,
With a seventh Book supplemental, is the poet's labour done,*

*All thy matchless deeds, O monarch, in this Lay will brighter shine,
List to us from first to ending if thy royal heart incline!*"

"Be it so," thus Rama answered, but the hours of day were o'er,
And Valmiki's youthful pupils to their cottage came once more.

Rama with his guests and courtiers slowly left the royal hall,
Eager was his heart to listen, eager were the monarchs all,

And the voice of song and music thus was lifted day to day,
And from day to day they listened to Valmiki's deathless Lay!

IV

Lava and Kusa Recognised

Flashed upon the contrite Rama glimpses of the dawning truth,
And with tears of love paternal Rama clasped each minstrel youth,

Yearned his sorrow-stricken bosom for his pure and peerless dame,
Sita banished to the forest, stainless in her righteous fame!

In his tears repentant Rama to Valmiki message sent,
That his heart with eager longing sought her from her banishment:

"Pure in soul! before these monarchs may she yet her virtue prove,
Grace once more my throne and kingdom, share my unforgotten love,

Pure in soul! before my subjects may her truth and virtue shine,
Queen of Rama's heart and empire may she once again be mine!"

V

Sita Lost

Morning dawned; and with Valmiki, Sita to the gathering came,
Banished wife and weeping mother, sorrow-stricken, suffering dame,

Pure in thought and deed, Valmiki, gave his troth and plighted word,—
Faithful still the banished Sita in her bosom held her lord!

"Mighty Saint," so Rama answered as he bowed his humbled head,
"Listening world will hear thy mandate and the word that thou hast said,

Never in his bosom Rama questioned Sita's faithful love,
And the God of Fire incarnate did her stainless virtue prove!

Pardon, if the voice of rumour drove me to a deed of shame,
Bowing to my people's wishes I disowned my sinless dame,

Pardon, if to please my subjects I have bade my Sita roam,
Tore her from my throne and empire, tore her from my heart and home!

In the dark and dreary forest was my Sita left to mourn,
In the lone and gloomy jungle were my royal children born,

Help me, Gods, to wipe this error and this deed of sinful pride,
May my Sita prove her virtue, be again my loving bride!"

Gods and Spirits, bright Immortals to that royal *Yajna* came,
Men of every race and nation, kings and chiefs of righteous fame,

Softly through the halls of splendour cool and scented breezes blew,
Fragrance of celestial blossoms o'er the royal chambers flew.

Sita saw the bright Celestials, monarchs gathered from afar,
Saw her royal lord and husband bright as heaven-ascending star,

Saw her sons as hermit-minstrels beaming with a radiance high,
Milk of love suffused her bosom, tear of sorrow filled her eye!

Rama's queen and Janak's daughter, will she stoop her cause to plead,
Witness of her truth and virtue can a loving woman need?

Oh! her woman's heart is bursting, and her day on earth is done,
And she pressed her heaving bosom, slow and sadly thus begun:

"*If unstained in thought and action I have lived from day of birth,
Spare a daughter's shame and anguish and receive her, Mother Earth!*

*If in duty and devotion I have laboured undefiled,
Mother Earth! who bore this woman, once again receive thy child!*

*If in truth unto my husband I have proved a faithful wife,
Mother Earth! relieve thy Sita from the burden of this life!*"

Then the earth was rent and parted, and a golden throne arose,
Held aloft by jewelled *Nagas* as the leaves enfold the rose,

And the Mother in embraces held her spotless sinless Child,
Saintly Janak's saintly daughter, pure and true and undefiled,

Gods and men proclaim her virtue! But fair Sita is no more,
Lone is Rama's loveless bosom and his days of bliss are o'er!

CONCLUSION

In the concluding portion of the *Uttara* or Supplemental Book, the descendants of Rama and his brothers are described as the founders of the great cities and kingdoms which flourished in Western India in the fourth and fifth centuries before the Christian Era.

Bharat had two sons, Taksha and Pushkala. The former founded Taksha-sila, to the east of the Indus, and known to Alexander and the Greeks as Taxila. The latter founded Pushkala-vati, to the west of the Indus, and known to Alexander and the Greeks as Peukelaotis. Thus the sons of Bharat are said to have founded kingdoms which flourished on either side of the Indus river in the fourth century before Christ.

Lakshman had two sons, Angada and Chandraketu. The former founded the kingdom of Karupada, and the latter founded the city of Chandrakanti in the Malwa country.

Satrughna had two sons, Suvahu and Satrughati. The former became king of Mathura, and the latter ruled in Vidisha.

Rama had two sons, Lava and Kusa. The former ruled in Sravasti, which was the capital of Oudh, at the time of the Buddha in the fifth and sixth centuries before Christ. The latter founded Kusavati at the foot of the Vindhya mountains.

The death of Rama and his brothers was in accordance with Hindu ideas of the death of the righteous. Lakshman died under somewhat peculiar circumstances. A messenger from heaven sought a secret conference with Rama, and Rama placed Lakshman at the gate, with strict injunctions that whoever intruded on the private conference should be slain. Lakshman himself had to disturb the conference by the solicitation of the celestial *rishi* Durvasa, who always appears on earth to create mischief. And true to the orders passed by Rama, he surrendered his life by penances, and went to heaven.

In the fulness of time, Rama and his other brothers left Ayodhya, crossed the Sarayu, surrendered their mortal life, and entered heaven.

EPILOGUE BY THE TRANSLATOR

Ancient India, like ancient Greece, boasts of two great Epics. The *Maha-bharata*, based on the legends and traditions of a great historical war, is the Iliad of India. The *Ramayana*, describing the wanderings and adventures of a prince banished from his country, has so far something in common with the Odyssey. Having placed before English readers a condensed translation of the Indian Iliad, I have thought it necessary to prepare the present condensed translation of the Indian Odyssey to complete the work. The two together comprise the whole of the Epic literature of the ancient Hindus; and the two together present us with the most graphic and life-like picture that exists of the civilisation and culture, the political and social life, the religion and thought of ancient India.

The *Ramayana*, like the *Maha-bharata*, is a growth of centuries, but the main story is more distinctly the creation of one mind. Among the many cultured races that flourished in Northern India about a thousand years before Christ, the Kosalas of Oudh and the Videhas of North Behar were perhaps the most cultured. Their monarchs were famed for their learning as well as for their prowess. Their priests distinguished themselves by founding schools of learning which were known all over India. Their sacrifices and gifts to the learned drew together the most renowned men of the age from distant regions. Their celebrated Universities (Parishads) were frequented by students from surrounding countries. Their compilations of the old *Vedic Hymns* were used in various parts of India. Their elaborate *Brahmanas* or Commentaries on the Vedas were handed down from generation to generation by priestly families. Their researches into the mysteries of the Soul, and into the nature of the One Universal Soul which pervades the creation, are still preserved in the ancient *Upanishads*, and are among the most valuable heritages which have been left to us by the ancients. And their researches and discoveries in science and philosophy gave them the foremost place among the gifted races of ancient India.

It would appear that the flourishing period of the Kosalas and the Videhas had already passed away, and the traditions of their prowess and learning had become a revered memory in India, when the poet composed the great Epic which perpetuates their fame. Distance of time lent a higher lustre to the achievements of these gifted races, and the age in which they flourished appeared to their descendants as the Golden Age of India. To the imagination of the poet, the age of the Kosalas and Videhas was associated with all that is great and glorious, all that is righteous and true. His description of Ayodhya, the capital town of the Kosalas, is a description of an ideal seat of righteousness. Dasa-ratha, the king of the Kosalas, is an ideal king, labouring for the good of a loyal people. Rama, the eldest son of Dasa-ratha and the hero of the Epic, is an ideal prince, brave and accomplished, devoted to his duty, unfaltering in his truth. The king of the Videhas, Janak (or rather Janaka, but I have omitted the final *a* of some names in this translation), is a monarch and a saint. Sita, the daughter of Janak and the heroine of the Epic, is the ideal of a faithful woman and a devoted wife. A pious reverence for the past pervades the great Epic; a lofty admiration of what is true and ennobling in the human character sanctifies the work; and delineations of the domestic life and the domestic virtues of the ancient Hindus, rich in tenderness and pathos, endear the picture to the hearts of the people of India to the present day.

It is probable that the first connected narrative of this Epic was composed within a few centuries after the glorious age of the Kosalas and the Videhas. But the work became so popular that it grew with age. It grew,—not like the *Maha-bharata* by the incorporation of new episodes, tales and traditions,—but by fresh descriptions of the same scenes and incidents. Generations of poets were never tired of adding to the description of scenes which were dear to the Hindu, and patient Hindu listeners were never tired of listening to such repetitions. The virtues of Rama and the faithfulness of Sita were described again and again in added lines and cantos. The grief of the old monarch at the banishment of the prince, and the sorrows of the mother at parting from her son, were depicted by succeeding versifiers in fresh verses. The loving devotion of Rama's brothers, the sanctity of saints, and the peacefulness of the hermitages visited by Rama, were described with endless reiteration. The long account of the grief of Rama at the loss of his wife, and stories of unending battles waged for her recovery, occupied generations of busy interpolators.

The *Sloka* verse in which much of the *Ramayana* is composed is the easiest of Sanscrit metres, and afforded a fatal facility to poets; and often we have the same scene, fully and amply described in one canto, repeated again in the two or three succeeding cantos. The unity of the composition is lost by these additions, and the effect of the narrative is considerably weakened by such endless repetition.

It would appear that the original work ended with the sixth Book, which describes the return of the hero to his country and to his loving subjects. The seventh Book is called *Uttara* or Supplemental, and in it we are told something of the dimensions of the poem, apparently after the fatal process of additions and interpolations had gone on for centuries. We are informed that the poem consists of six Books and a Supplemental Book; and that it comprises 500 cantos and 24,000 couplets. And we are also told in this Supplemental Book that the descendants of Rama and his brothers founded some of the great towns and states which, we know from other sources, flourished in the fifth and fourth centuries before Christ. It is probable therefore that the Epic, commenced after 1000 B.C., had assumed something like its present shape a few centuries before the Christian Era.

The foregoing account of the genesis and growth of the *Ramayana* will indicate in what respects it resembles the *Maha-bharata*, and in what respects the two Indian Epics differ from each other. The *Maha-bharata* grew out of the legends and traditions of a great historical war between the Kurus and the Panchalas; the *Ramayana* grew out of the recollections of the golden age of the Kosalas and the Videhas. The characters of the *Maha-bharata* are characters of flesh and blood, with the virtues and crimes of great actors in the historic world; the characters of the *Rama-*

yana are more often the ideals of manly devotion to truth, and of womanly faithfulness and love in domestic life. The poet of the *Maha-bharata* relies on the real or supposed incidents of a war handed down from generation to generation in songs and ballads, and weaves them into an immortal work of art; the poet of the *Ramayana* conjures up the memories of a golden age, constructs lofty ideals of piety and faith, and describes with infinite pathos domestic scenes and domestic affections which endear the work to modern Hindus. As a heroic poem the *Maha-bharata* stands on a higher level; as a poem delineating the softer emotions of our everyday life the *Ramayana* sends its roots deeper into the hearts and minds of the million in India.

These remarks will be probably made clearer by a comparison of what may be considered parallel passages in the two great Epics. In heroic description, the bridal of Sita is poor and commonplace, compared with the bridal of Draupadi with all the bustle and tumult of a real contest among warlike suitors. The rivalry between Rama and Ravan, between Lakshman and Indrajit, is feeble in comparison with the life-long jealousy and hatred which animated Arjun and Karna, Bhima and Duryodhan. Sita's protest and defiance, spoken to Ravan when he carried her away, lack the fire and the spirit of Draupadi's appeal on the occasion when she was insulted in court. The Council of War held by Ravan is a poor affair in comparison with the Council of War held by Yudhisthir in the Matsya kingdom. And Bibhishan's final appeal for peace and Ravan's scornful reply will scarcely compare with the sublime eloquence with which Krishna implored the old monarch of the Kurus not to plunge into a disastrous war, and the deep determination with which Duryodhan replied:—

> "Town nor village, mart nor hamlet, help us righteous Gods in heaven,
> Spot that needle's point can cover shall not unto them be given!"

In the whole of the *Ramayana* there is no character with the fiery determination and the deep-seated hatred for the foe which inspire Karna or Arjun, Bhima or Duryodhan. And in the unending battles waged by Rama and his allies there is no incident so stirring, so animated, so thrilling, as the fall of Abhimanyu, the vengeance of Arjun, the final contest between Arjun and Karna, or the final contest between Bhima and Duryodhan. The whole tenor of the *Ramayana* is subdued and calm, pacific and pious; the whole tenor of the *Maha-bharata* is warlike and spirited.

And yet, without rivalling the heroic grandeur of the *Maha-bharata*, the *Ramayana* is immeasurably superior in its delineation of those softer and perhaps deeper emotions which enter into our everyday life, and hold the world together. And these descriptions, essentially of Hindu life, are yet so true to nature that they apply to all races and nations.

There is something indescribably touching and tender in the description of the love of Rama for his subjects and the loyalty of his people towards Rama,—that loyalty which has ever been a part of the Hindu character in every age—

"As a father to his children to his loving men he came,
Blessed our homes and maids and matrons till our infants lisped his name,
For our humble woes and troubles Rama hath the ready tear,
To our humble tales of suffering Rama lends his willing ear!"

Deeper than this was Rama's duty towards his father and his father's fondness for Rama; and the portion of the Epic which narrates the dark scheme by which the prince was at last torn from the heart and home of his dying father is one of the most powerful and pathetic passages in Indian literature. The stepmother of Rama, won by the virtues and the kindliness of the prince, regards his proposed coronation with pride and pleasure, but her old nurse creeps into her confidence like a creeping serpent, and envenoms her heart with the poison of her own wickedness. She arouses the slumbering jealousy of a woman and awakens the alarms of a mother, till—

"Like a slow but deadly poison worked the ancient nurse's tears,
And a wife's undying impulse mingled with a mother's fears!"

The nurse's dark insinuations work on the mind of the queen till she becomes a desperate woman, resolved to maintain her own influence on her husband, and to see her own son on the throne. The determination of the young queen tells with terrible effect on the weakness and vacillation of the feeble old monarch, and Rama is banished at last. And the scene closes with a pathetic story in which the monarch recounts his misdeed of past years, accepts his present suffering as the fruit of that misdeed, and dies in agony for his banished son. The inner workings of the human heart and of human motives, the dark intrigue of a scheming dependant, the awakening jealousy and alarm of a wife and a mother, the determination of a woman and an imperious queen, and the feebleness and despair and death of a fond old father and husband, have never been more vividly described. Shakespeare himself has not depicted the workings of stormy passions in the human heart more graphically or more vividly, with greater truth or with more terrible power.

It is truth and power in the depicting of such scenes, and not in the delineation of warriors and warlike incidents, that the *Ramayana* excels. It is in the delineation of domestic incidents, domestic affections and domestic jealousies, which are appreciated by the prince and the peasant alike, that the *Ramayana* bases its appeal to the hearts of the million in India. And beyond all this, the righteous devotion of Rama, and the faithfulness and womanly love of Sita, run like two threads of gold through the whole fabric of the Epic, and ennoble and sanctify the work in the eyes of Hindus.

Rama and Sita are the Hindu ideals of a Perfect Man and a Perfect Woman; their truth under trials and temptations, their endurance under privations, and their devotion to duty under all vicissitudes of fortune, form the Hindus ideal of a Perfect Life. In this respect the *Ramayana* gives us a true picture of Hindu faith and righteous life as Dante's "Divine Comedy" gives us a picture of the faith and belief of the Middle Ages in Europe. Our own ideals in the present day may not be the ideals of the tenth century before Christ or the fourteenth century after Christ; but mankind will not willingly let die those great creations of the past which shadow forth the ideals and beliefs of interesting periods in the progress of human civilisation.

Sorrow and suffering, trial and endurance, are a part of the

Hindu ideal of a Perfect Life of righteousness. Rama suffers for fourteen years in exile, and is chastened by privations and misfortunes, before he ascends the throne of his father. In a humble way this course of training was passed through by every pious Hindu of the ancient times. Every Aryan boy in India was taken away from his parents at an early age, and lived the hard life of an anchorite under his teacher for twelve or twenty-four or thirty-six years, before he entered the married life and settled down as a house-holder. Every Aryan boy assumed the rough garment and the staff and girdle of a student, lived as a mendicant and begged his food from door to door, attended on his preceptor as a menial, and thus trained himself in endurance and suffering as well as in the traditional learning of the age, before he became a house-holder. The pious Hindu saw in Rama's life the ideal of a true Hindu life, the success and the triumph which follow upon endurance and faith and devotion to duty. It is the truth and endurance of Rama under sufferings and privations which impart the deepest lessons to the Hindu character, and is the highest ideal of a Hindu righteous life. The ancient ideal may seem to us far-fetched in these days, but we can never fully comprehend the great moral Epic of the Hindus unless we endeavour to study fully and clearly its relations to old Hindu ideas and old Hindu life.

And if trial and endurance are a part of a Hindu's ideal of a man's life, devotion and self-abnegation are still more essentially a part of his ideal of a woman's life. Sita holds a place in the hearts of women in India which no other creation of a poet's imagination holds among any other nation on earth. There is not a Hindu woman whose earliest and tenderest recollections do not cling round the story of Sita's sufferings and Sita's faithfulness, told in the nursery, taught in the family circle, remembered and cherished through life. Sita's adventures in a desolate forest and in a hostile prison only represent in an exaggerated form the humbler trials of a woman's life: and Sita's endurance and faithfulness teach her devotion to duty in all trials and troubles of life. "For," said Sita :—

"For my mother often taught me and my father often spake,
That her home the wedded woman doth beside her husband make,

As the shadow to the substance, to her lord is faithful wife,
And she parts not from her consort till she parts with fleeting life!
Therefore bid me seek the jungle and in pathless forests roam,
Where the wild deer freely ranges and the tiger makes his home,
Happier than a father's mansions in the woods will Sita rove,
Waste no thought on home or kindred, nestling in her husband's love!"

The ideal of life was joy and beauty and gladness in ancient Greece; the ideal of life was piety and endurance and devotion in ancient India. The tale of Helen was a tale of womanly beauty and loveliness which charmed the western world. The tale of Sita was a tale of womanly faith and self-abnegation which charmed and fascinated the Hindu world. Repeated trials bring out in brighter relief the unfaltering truth of Sita's character; she goes to a second banishment in the woods with the same trust and devotion to her lord as before, and she returns once more, and sinks into the bosom of her Mother Earth, true in death as she had been true in life. The creative imagination of the Hindus has conceived no loftier and holier character than Sita; the literature of the world has not produced a higher ideal of womanly love, womanly truth, and womanly devotion.

The modern reader will now comprehend why India produced, and has preserved for well-nigh three thousand years, two Epics instead of one national Epic. No work of the imagination abides long unless it is animated by some sparks of imperishable truth, unless it truly embodies some portion of our human feelings, human faith and human life. The *Maha-bharata* depicts the political life of ancient India, with all its valour and heroism, ambition and lofty chivalry. The *Ramayana* embodies the domestic and religious life of ancient India, with all its tenderness and sweetness, its endurance and devotion. The one picture without the other were incomplete; and we should know but little of the ancient Hindus if we did not comprehend their inner life and faith as well as their political life and their warlike virtues. The two together give us a true and graphic picture of ancient Indian life and civilisation;

and no nation on earth has preserved a more faithful picture of its glorious past.

In condensing the *Ramayana* with its more than 24,000 Sanscrit couplets into 2000 English couplets I have followed the same plan which was adopted in my translation of the *Maha-bharata*. I have selected those sections or cantos which tell the leading incidents of the Epic, and have translated the whole or main portions of them, and these selected passages are linked together by short notes. The plan, as was explained before, has this advantage, that the story is told not by the translator in his own way, but by the poet himself; the passages placed before the reader are not the translator's abridgment of a long poem, but selected passages from the poem itself. It is the ancient poet of India, and not the translator, who narrates the old story; but he narrates only such portions of it as describe the leading incidents. We are told that the sons of Rama recited the whole poem of 24,000 verses, divided into 500 cantos or sections, in twenty-five days. The modern reader has not the patience of the Hindu listener of the old school; but a selection of the leading portions of that immortal song arranged in 2000 verses and in 84 short sections, may possibly receive a hearing, even from the much-distracted modern reader.

While speaking of my own translation I must not fail to make some mention of my predecessors in this work. The magnificent edition of the *Ramayana* (Bengal recension) published with an Italian translation by Gorresio, at the expense of Charles Albert, King of Sardinia in 1843-67, first introduced this great Epic to the European public; and it was not long before M. Hippolyte Fauche presented the European world with a French translation of this edition. The Benares recension of the *Ramayana* has since been lithographed in Bombay, and a printed edition of the same recension with Ramanuja's commentary was brought out by the venerable Hem Chandra Vidyaratna in Calcutta in 1869-85. The talented and indefatigable Mr. Ralph Griffith, C.I.E., who has devoted a lifetime to translating Indian poetry into English, has produced an almost complete translation of the first six Books in more than 24,000 English couplets, and has given an abstract of the seventh Book in prose. And a complete translation of the *Ramayana* into English prose has since appeared in Calcutta.

The object of the present work is very different from that of these meritorious editions and translations. The purpose of this work, as explained above, is not to attempt a complete translation of a voluminous Epic, but to place before the general reader the leading story of that Epic by translating a number of selected passages and connecting them together by short notes. The purpose of this volume is not to repeat the long poem which Rama's sons are supposed to have recited in 24,000 Sanscrit couplets, but only to narrate the main incidents of that poem within the reasonable limit of 2000 verses. And the general reader who seeks for a practical acquaintance with the great Indian poem within a reasonable compass will, it is hoped, find in this book a handy and not unacceptable translation of the leading story of the Epic.

I have stated before that in India, the *Ramayana* is still a living tradition and a living faith. It forms the basis of the moral instruction of a nation, and it is a part of the lives of two hundred millions of people. It is necessary to add that when the modern languages of India were first formed out of the ancient Sanscrit and Prakrits, in the ninth and tenth centuries after Christ, the *Ramayana* had the greatest influence in inspiring our modern poets and forming our modern tongues. Southern India took the lead, and a translation of the *Ramayana* in the Tamil language appeared as early as 1100 A.D. Northern India and Bengal and Bombay followed the example; Tulsi Das's *Ramayana* is the great classic of the Hindi language, Krittibas's *Ramayana* is a classic in the Bengali language, and Sridhar's *Ramayana* is a classic in the Mahratta language. Generations of Hindus in all parts of India have studied the ancient story in these modern translations; they have heard it recited in the houses of the rich; and they have seen it acted on the stage at religious festivals in every great town and every populous village through the length and breadth of India.

More than this, the story of Rama has inspired our religious reformers, and purified the popular faith of our modern times. Rama, the true and dutiful, was accepted as the Spirit of God descended on earth, as an incarnation of Vishnu the Preserver of the World. The great teacher Ramanuja proclaimed the monotheism of Vishnu in Southern India in the twelfth century; the reformer Ramananda proclaimed the same faith in Northern India in the thirteenth or fourteenth century; and his follower, the gifted Kabir conceived the bold idea of uniting Hindus and Mahomedans in the worship of One God. "The God of the Hindus," he said, "is the God of the Mahomedans, be he invoked as *Rama* or *Ali*." "The city of the Hindu God is Benares, and the city of the Mahomedan God is Mecca; but search your hearts, and there you will find the God both of Hindus and Mahomedans." "If the Creator dwells in tabernacles, whose dwelling is the universe?"

The reformer Chaitanya preached the same sublime monotheism in Bengal, and the reformer Nanak in the Punjab, in the sixteenth century. And down to the present day the popular mind in India, led away by the worship of many images in many temples, nevertheless holds fast to the cardinal idea of One God, and believes the heroes of the ancient Epics—*Krishna* and *Rama*—to be the incarnations of that God. The various sects of the Hindus, specially the sects of Vishnu and of Siva who form the great majority of the people, quarrel about a name as they often did in Europe in the Middle Ages, and each sect gives to the Deity the special name by which the sect is known. In the teeming villages of Bengal, in the ancient shrines of Northern India, and far away in the towns and hamlets of Southern India, the prevailing faith of the million is a popular monotheism underlying the various ceremonials in honour of various images and forms,—and that popular monotheism generally recognises the heroes of the two ancient Epics,—*Krishna* and *Rama*, as the earthly incarnations of the great God who pervades and rules the universe.

To know the Indian Epics is to understand the Indian people better. And to trace the influence of the Indian Epics on the life and civilisation of the nation, and on the development of their modern languages, literatures, and religious reforms, is to comprehend the real history of the people during three thousand years.

UNIVERSITY COLLEGE, LONDON
13th August, 1899

ROMESH DUTT